ELECTRONICS MECHANIC FIRST YEAR MCQ

OBJECTIVE QUESTION ANSWERS

MANOJ DOLE

Digitization is the need of the time. In the future, training in industrial training institutes will need to be conducted using online internet to make training more convenient and easy. E-books containing a set of MCQ questions will be made available to the trainees as they need to be more accustomed to the multiple choice questions MCQ to prepare for the online exams taking place in their industrial training institutes.

With all these factors in mind, Mr. Manoj Madhukar Dole Instructor, Industrial Training Institute, Satara, has written books according to the new annual system and NSQF-5 syllabus. And they've created theoretical mobile apps and blogs to make training easier, and made all these educational materials available for download on the world famous websites Google Play Store, Amazon and Apple Book Store.

The books were published by Hon'ble Joint Director Shri Rajendra Ghume Saheb Regional Office of Vocational Education and Training, Pune on 9/1/2019, at this time Shri Prakash Saigavkar Saheb Principal Government Industrial Training Institute Aundh Pune, Shri Tukaram Misal Saheb Principal Govt. Q. Sanstha Satara, Shri Sachin Dhumal Saheb District Vocational Education and Training Officer Satara, Shri Yatin Pargaonkar Saheb Principal Govt. Q. Sanstha Kolhapur, Shri Vikas Teke Saheb Inspector Vocational Education and Training Regional Office Pune, Palekar Foods Products Pvt. Ltd. Entrepreneurial Chairman of Satara Mr. Nilkanthrao Palekar Saheb, Chairman of Hira Foods Mr. Ibrahim Baba Tamboli Saheb, Mrs. Shalmali Pawar Headmaster Government Technical School Center Satara and other dignitaries were present on the occasion.

Contents

Prologue *vii*

Foreword *ix*

Preface *xi*

Acknowledgements *xiii*

1. Electronics Mechanic First Year Qr Code Images 1

2. Electronics Mechanic First Year Mcq 16

Prologue

Electronics Mechanic First Year MCQ is a simple Book for ITI & Engineering Course **Electronics Mechanic** First Year, Revised NSQF Syllabus in 2022, It contains objective questions with underlined & bold correct answers MCQ covering all topics including all about the latest & Important about safety and environment, use of fire extinguishers, artificial respiratory resuscitation to begin with. He gets the idea of trade tools & its standardization, Familiarize with basics of electricity, test the cable and measure the electrical parameter. Skilling practice on different types & combination of cells for operation and maintenance of batteries being done. Identify and test passive and active electronic components. Construct and test unregulated and regulated power supplies. Practice soldering and de-soldering of various types of electrical and electronic components on through hole PCBs. Assemble a computer system, install OS, Practice with MS office. Use the internet, browse, create mail IDs, download desired data from internet using search engines. construct and test amplifier, oscillator and wave shaping circuits. Testing of power electronic components. Construct and test power control circuits. Identify and test opto electronic devices. Able to achieve the skill on SMD Soldering and De-soldering of discrete SMD components. Verifying the truth tables of various digital ICs by referring Data book. Practice circuit simulation software to simulate and test various circuits. Identify various types of LEDs, LED displays and interface them to a digital counter and test. Construct and test various circuits using linear ICs 741 & 555, and lots more.

We add new question answers with each new version. Please email us in case of any errors/omissions. This is arguably the largest and best e-Book for All engineering multiple choice questions and answers.

As a student you can use it for your exam prep. This e-Book is also useful for professors to refresh material.

Foreword

Vocational education and training is imparted through the Department of Vocational Education and Training through the Department of Business Education and Business Practical to supply multi-skilled artisans in line with the rapidly growing demand in the industrial sector in the 21st century. All the occupations within the institutions are important, as the trainees from these occupations develop multi-skills as per the demands of the industry.

with the noble intention of making available MCQ e-books suitable for all businesses, considering that all the examinations in all the industries in the industrial sector are conducted online and include MCQ method questions. Mr. Manoj Madhukar Dole has written a very good e-book on MCQ method as per the new annual syllabus. This e-book will definitely be a guide for all the trainees, trainee candidates, training instructors and others concerned.

The author of the book is Mr. Manoj Madhukar Dole, Instructor Gov. ITI Satara has 17 years of training experience. Written as a new annual pattern, this e-book incorporates modern digital QR Code technology to understand the layout, simple language, and simple syntax, diagrams and videos for each subject. So I am sure that this e-book will definitely be useful for in-depth study and exam practice. The work they have done is certainly commendable.

Mr. Tukaram Misal
Principal Government Industrial Training Institute Satara.

Preface

DGET New Delhi and CSTARI Kolkata have been implementing an annual pattern for all businesses in ITI since the August 2018 session. The examination system will also be changed and it will be online from this year and since all the questions are of Objective Type (MCQ), the trainees are in dire need of in-depth study. It is with this in mind that we are delighted to present the books based on the old NIMI pattern and a complete overview of the new annual pattern, and we hope that these books will be a guide for all business directors and trainees. Is.

For writing these books, Johar Awate Saheb, Principal of ITI Akluj. Former Principal of ITI Satara Saigavkar Saheb, Assistant Director Shri Chandrakant Dhekne Saheb Regional Office of Vocational Education and Training, Pune, District Vocational Education and Training Officer Sachin Dhumal Saheb and Headmaster Government Technical School Kendra Shalmali Pawar Madam and son Adhiraj Dole, mother Kusum Dole, I am very grateful to my father Madhukar Dole and wife Ashwini Dole for their special guidance and cooperation from time to time.

Also, in a very short period of time, the book was reviewed by Shri Rajendra Ghume Saheb, Joint Director, Vocational Education and Training Regional Office, Pune, for his invaluable time in publishing the book. I am sincerely grateful for their feedback.

I am grateful to the Instructor of ITI Satara for there continuous support from the very beginning of writing the book.

From this book, I consider myself blessed to have shared my thoughts on e-learning with you. I will not claim that this book is perfect, because considering the perfection, this book is an attempt and is in its infancy. They will be valuable for improvement if they are tested and suggested.

Manoj Dole
Dated 9/1/2019

Acknowledgements

The industrial training and theoretical examination system of our industrial training institutes and these changes have been accepted by the craft instructors and the trainees. Theoretical examinations conducted in your industrial training institutes are also conducted online. Since these examinations are of multiple choice MCQ method, the trainees will need to get more practice of such questions.

With all these considerations in mind, Mr. Manoj Madhukar, Director, Dole Crafts, Katari Industrial Training Institute, Satara, has done a thorough study and with his diligent work and added his keen intellect, according to the new annual system and NSQF-5 syllabus, e-book of Katari and other machine trades. -Book) and they have created mobile apps and blogs on theoretical topics to make training easier and have made all these educational materials available for download on the world famous websites Google Play Store, Amazon and Apple Book Store. Training has been made easier by creating a print version and using advanced techniques like QR Code.

All these educational materials will definitely be a guide for all the trainees for in-depth study and for the craft instructors and other concerned who are imparting vocational training.

CHAPTER ONE

Electronics Mechanic First Year QR Code Images

Download App
Online Test Exam
ITI Books
AutoCAD CAM
JOB & Apprentice
Online Theory
Computer Course
Trading Course
CNC Course
MSCIT Course
Shopping Business
Internet Business
Web Designing
Online Services
Top Sportsmans
Indian Army
Freedom Fighters
Top Scientists
Social Reformers
Motivational Speaker
Top Richest People
Join WhatsApp Group
Join Facebook Group
Like Facebook Page
PAN / Adhar / Licence Passport

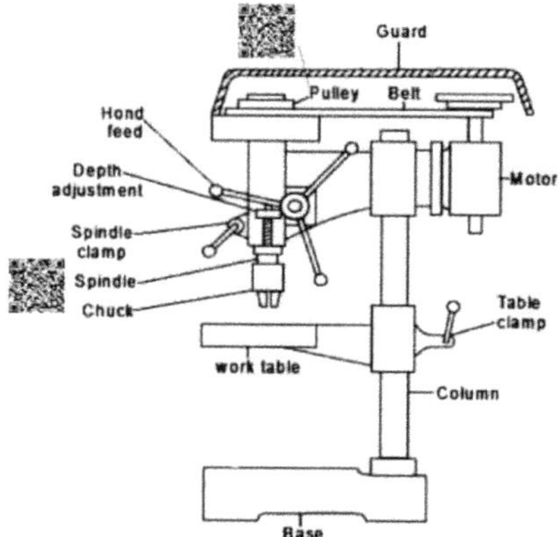

Piller Drilling Machine

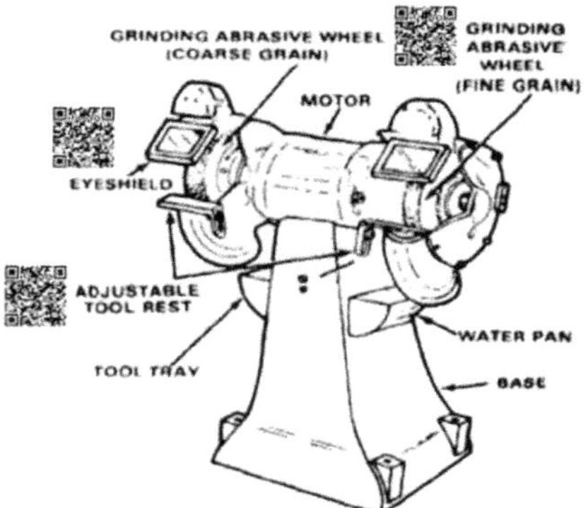

Pedastal Grinding Machine

14 ITI Book MCQ - Manoj Dole
www.itibook.com
battery
capacitor
cell
dynamometer
electromagnet
heater
inductance
magnet
www.itigov.blogspot.com www.jobapprentices.blogspot.com www.ititests.blogspot.com
www.itibook.com

15 ITI Book MCQ - Manoj Dole
www.itibook.com
megger
motor
multimeter
ohmmeter
resistores
star connected
alternator
voltmeter
ammeter
wattmeter
www.itigov.blogspot.com www.jobapprentices.blogspot.com www.ititests.blogspot.com
www.itibook.com

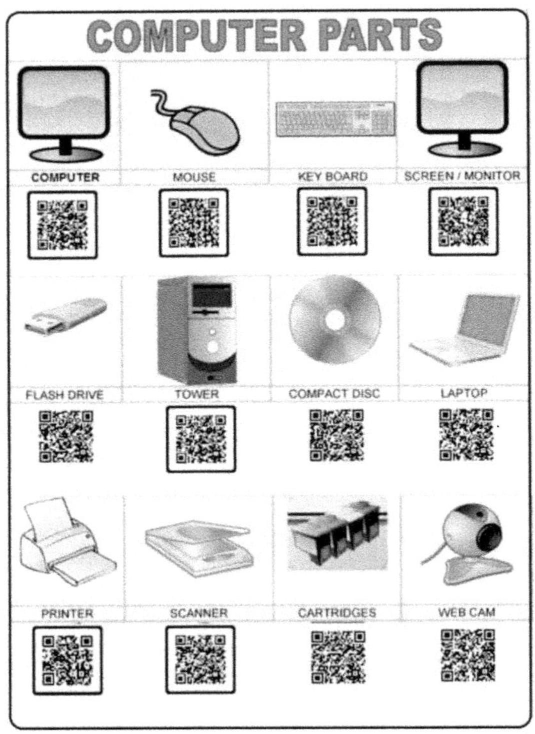
COMPUTER PARTS
COMPUTER
MOUSE
KEY BOARD
SCREEN / MONITOR
FLASH DRIVE
TOWER
COMPACT DISC
LAPTOP
PRINTER
SCANNER
CARTRIDGES
WEB CAM

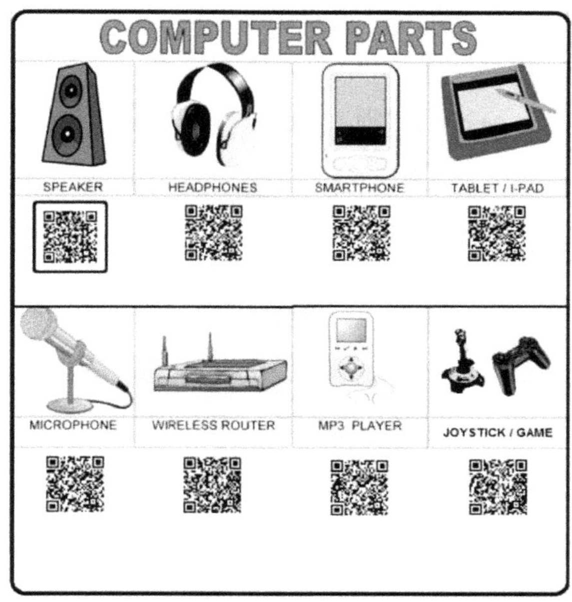
COMPUTER PARTS
SPEAKER
HEADPHONES
SMARTPHONE
TABLET / I-PAD
MICROPHONE
WIRELESS ROUTER
MP3 PLAYER
JOYSTICK / GAME

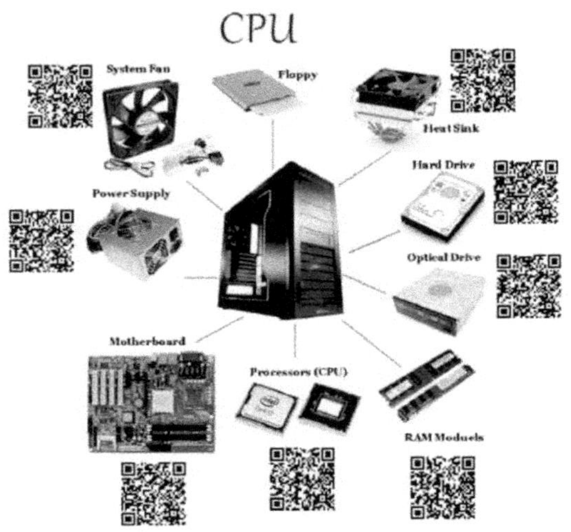

Computer CPU
Hardware Components

Motherboard
Hardware Components

Learn DOS Commands
All DOS Command with explanations
MS-DOS
Computer
Operator

topic
Microsoft Access

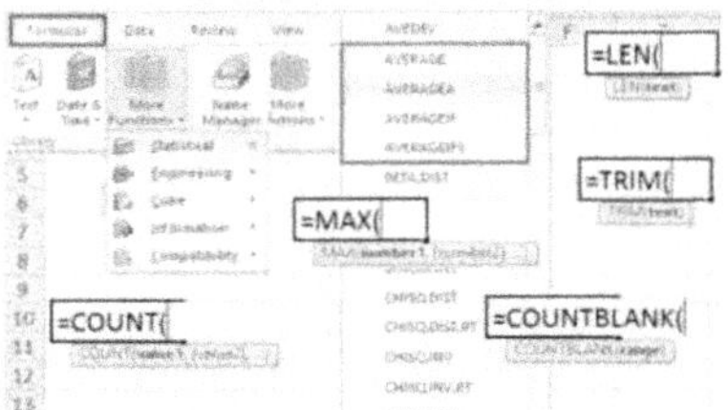
Excel Basic Functions
=LEN(
=TRIM(
=MAX(
=COUNT(
=COUNTBLANK(

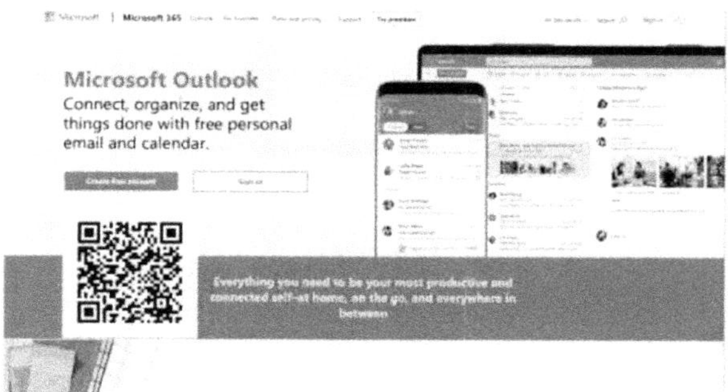
Microsoft Outlook
Connect, organize, and get things done with free personal email and calendar.
Everything you need to be your most productive and connected self-at home, on the go, and everywhere in between

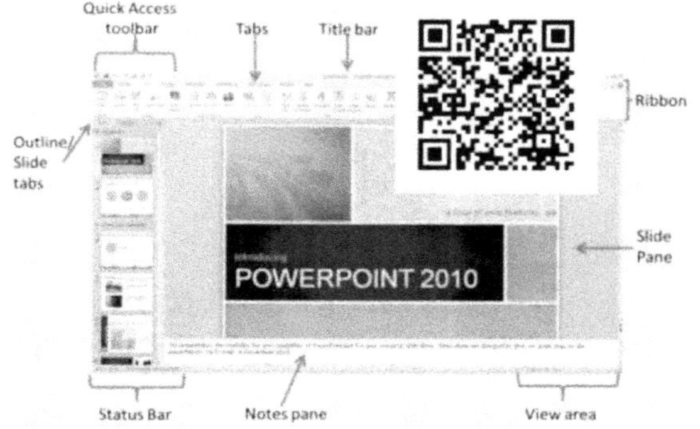
Quick Access toolbar
Tabs
Title bar
Ribbon
Outline/ Slide tabs
Slide Pane
POWERPOINT 2010
Status Bar
Notes pane
View area

MS Paint

Microsoft
FEATURES OF
MS WORD
IN HINDI
• WHAT IS MS WORD
• HISTORY OF MS WORD
• FEATURES OF MS WORD

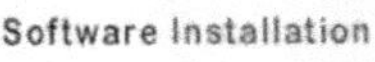
Software Installation

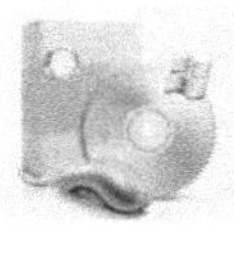

CDBurnerXP

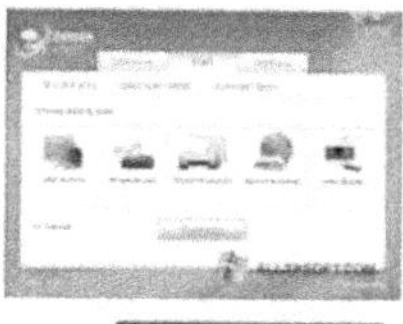

Top Linux OS

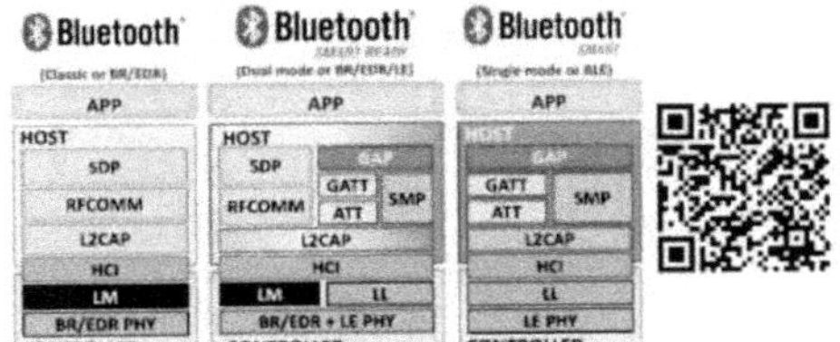
Bluetooth
APP
HOST
SDP
RFCOMM
L2CAP
HCI
LM
BR/EDR PHY
CONTROLLER
Bluetooth
APP
HOST
SDP
GAP
GATT
ATT
SMP
RFCOMM
L2CAP
HCI
LM
LL
BR/EDR + LE PHY
CONTROLLER
Bluetooth
APP
HOST
GAP
GATT
ATT
SMP
L2CAP
HCI
LL
LE PHY
CONTROLLER

Wi Fi
DSL/Cable
Local Network

What is a Browser - Definition and

What is
Email?

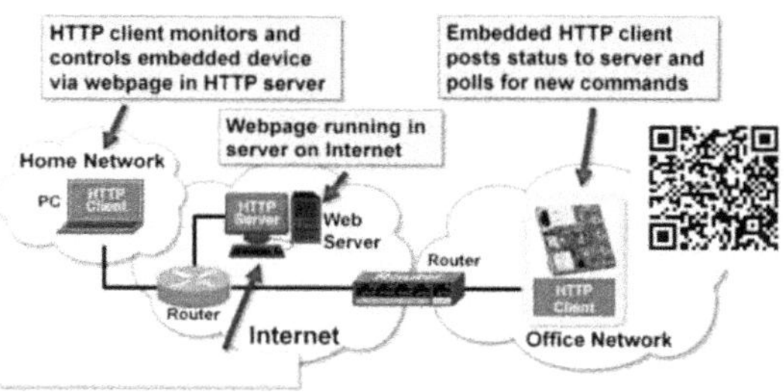
HTTP client monitors and
controls embedded device
via webpage in HTTP server
Embedded HTTP client
posts status to server and
polls for new commands
Webpage running in
server on Internet
Home Network
PC
HTTP Client
HTTP Server
Web
Server
Router
Router
HTTP Client
Internet
Office Network

CHAPTER TWO

Electronics Mechanic First Year MCQ

1] Which one is a workshop safety?

A] Keep shop floor clean and free from grease, oil or other slippery materials

B] Stop the machine before changing the speed

C] Don't use cracked or chipped tools

D] Don't try to stop a running machine with hand

2] In Personal Protect Equipment (PPE] HELMET is used to

A] protect head

B] Protect eyes

C] Protect hands

D] Protect ears

3] Which of the following belongs to general safety?

A Have a worker in good attitude

B] The work clean and clear

C] Concentrate on your work

D] Keep the floor and gangways clean and clear

4] While grinding, which is used to protect the eyes?

A] Dark green glass

B] Mask

C] Sun glasses

D] Safety goggles

5] Which of the following is done for machine safety?

A] Check the oil level before starting the machine

B] Do things in a methodical way

C] Keep the floor and gangways clean and clear

D] Don't use dies and scarves

6] In Personal Protect Equipment (PPE], 'sleeves' is used to protect ----------

A] Face

B] Eyes

C] Ears

<u>D] Hands</u>

7] ABC stands for --------------

A] Automatic Breathing Control

B] Automatic Blood Control

<u>C] Airway Breathing Circulation</u>

D] Automatic Blood Circulation

8] Fire & FIRE EXTINGUISHERS

Fire extinguisher

9] To put off"Class B" fire, the types of fire extinguisher used is ....

<u>A] dry power</u>

B] Carbon dioxide

C] Jet of water

D] Foam type

10] Which type of fire extinguisher is used to put off general fire?

<u>A] Water type Extinguisher</u>

B] Foam type Extinguisher

C] Dry chemical powder Extinguisher

D] Carbon dioxide (C02] Extinguisher

11] In case of bleeding, take treatment Of

D] cold 3" and rest

<u>A] spray cold water</u>

B] Bandage immediately -----.

B] Enquire about the accident thought treatment

12] in case of an accident, the victim should im

A] Asked to take rest

C] Attended immediately

D] leave him

13] First aid is given to an injured or ill person primarily....

A] Save life

B] Prevent further deterioration of the muff's

C] Give best possible comfort

D] All of these

14] Colour code for Bins for waste paper segregation is -----

A] blue Colour

B] Yellow Colour

C] Red Colour

D] Green Colour

15] In Japanese Seiko stands for -------------

A] Shine

B] Sort

C] Standardize

D] Sustain

16] Benefit of SS system is ------

A] Increase in productivity

B] Increase in quality

C] Reduction in wastage of time

D] All of these

17] Safety is -----------

A] nobody's business

B] every bodise business

C] Some bodies business

D] The organization business

18] For basic categories of safety signs are available The meaning of"prohibition" sign ----

A] shows it must not be done
B] Shows what must be done
C] Warns the hazard or danger
D] Gives information of safety provision
18] One micrometer (U] is equal to...
A] 0.1mm
B] 0.01mm
C] 0.001mm
D] 0.0001mm
19] The caliper meant for measuring the width of a slot is...
A] Odd leg caliper
B] Outside caliper
C] Jenny caliper
D] Inside calliper

Calliper

20] The size of the dividers are specified by the -----------
A] Total length of legs
B] Distance between the points when fully opened
C] Length of legs without points
D] distance between the pivot and the point
21] The instrument used to mark parallel lines, parallel to the datum edge is -
A] jenny caliper
B] Divider
C] Outside calliper
D] Inside calliper
22] Which one of the following is an indirect measuring tool?
A] Outside caliper
B] Vernier calliper
C] Steel rule

D] Outside micrometer

23] For cutting thin tubing, the most suitable pitch of the hacksaw blade is...

A] 1.8mm

B] 1.4mm

C] 1mm

D] 0.8mm

24] For cutting solid brass, the most suitable pitch of the hacksaw blade is...

A] 1.8mm

B] 1.4mm

C] 1mm

D] 0.8mm

Hacksaw frame

25] A new hacksaw blade after a few strokes becomes loose because of the...

A] Stretching of the blade

B] Wing-nut threads being worn out

C] Wrong pitch of the blade

D] Improper selection of the set of saws.

26] While cutting small diameter pipes, it is advisable to watch regularly and ensure that...

A] The cut is along the curved line

B] More saw teeth are in contract

C] The work is not overheated

D] Proper balancing of hacksaw is maintained

27] The vice clamps are used to...

A] Protect hard jaws

B] Clamp the work pieces rigidly

C] <u>Protect the finished surfaces</u>

D] Prevent the movable jaw being filed

28] The reference surface during marking is provided by the...

A] Surface gauge

B] Workpiece

C] Drawing of the work

D] <u>Marking table surface</u>

29] The size of an engineer's vice is specified by the...

A] Length of the movable jaw

B] <u>Width of the jaws</u>

C] Height of the vice

D] Maximum opening of the jaws

30] The part of the universal surface gauge which helps to draw a parallel line along a datum edge is the..

A] Rocker arm

B] Snug

C] Fine adjustment screw

D] <u>Guide pins</u>

Universal surface guage

31] Scribers are made of...

A] Mild steel

B] <u>High carbon steel</u>

C] Brass

D] Cast iron

32] Portion of the hammer used for fixing the handle is...

A] Face

B] Peen

C] Cheek

D] Eye hole

33] Weight of the hammer for the marking purpose is...

A] 250g

B] 500g

C] 1 kg

D] 2 kgs

Hammer

34] The size of the dividers are specified by the...

A] Total length of the legs

B] Distance between the points when fully opened

C] Length of legs without the points

D] Distance between the pivot and the point

35] The included angle of the groove of 'V' block is always....

A] 45°

B] 60°

C] 90°

D] 120°

36] 'V' blocks are available in grades of...

A] A & B

B] A,B & C

C] 1,2 & 3

D] 1 & 2

37] 'V' blocks of grade 'B' are made of

A] Cast iron

B] Mild steel

C] Steel

D] Cast steel

38] Name the punch used to locate the centre.

A] Prick punch 30°

B] Prick punch 60°

C] Centre punch

D] Dot punch

Centre punch

39] The point angle of centre punch is --------

A] 30°

B] 50°

c] 900

D] 1200

40] Punches are used for forming ---------of any shape

A] Holes

B] Mining

C] Knurling

D] Reaming

41] Generally the length of the handle of the vice is ----------

A] 1.5 times the normal size of the vice

B] 2.5 times the normal size of the vice

C] 3.5 times the normal size of the vice

D] 4.5 times the normal size of the vice

Bench vice

42] Bench vice spindle is made of ....

A] mild steel

B] Cast iron

C] Tool steel

D] Bronze

43] The convexity of files helps...

A] To file concave surfaces

B] To file convex surfaces

C] To prevent rounding of edges of work

D] The file to become straight when pressure is applied

Files

44] Which file used for filling wood, leather and other soft material? .

A] Single cut file

B] Double cut file

c] Rasp cut file

D] Curved cut file

45] File used is used for ------------

A] Cleaning the work piece

C] Renewing the file teeth

B] cleaning the file teeth

D] Cleaning the chips

46] File card is used to --------

A] Clean the work piece

C] Renew the file teeth

B] Clean the file teeth

47] The point angle of scriber is -----------

A] 30°

B] 60°

C] 5° to 10°

D] 12° to 15°

48] The cutting angle for chipping cast iron is...

A] 37.5°

B] 55°

C] 60°

D] 90°

49] The chisel will dig into the material when...

A] The rake angle is more

B] The clearance angle is too low

C] The angle of inclination is more

D] The angle of inclination is too low

50] A slight convexity is given to the cutting edge to...

A] Cut curved surfaces

B] Cut sharp corners

C] Prevent digging of the ends

D] Allow the lubricant to enter

51] Surface plates are made of...

A] High grade cast steel

B] Fine-grained cast iron

C] Alloy steels

D] Wrought iron

52] Surface plates are specified by their length and breadth & are in

A] decimetre

B] Cubic meter

C] Cylindrical

53] Ribs are given on the unmachined portion of the angle plate for...

A] Easy handling

B] Convenience in manufacturing

C] Clamping while setting on machines

D] Rigidity and to prevent distortion

54] The slots on the angle plate are given for...

A] Reducing weight

B] Aligning the work

C] Lifting using hooks

D] Accommodating bolts.

55] The size of the angle plates is stated by...

A] Weight

B] Length

C] Length x width

D] Size number

1. The S.I. unit of power is

(a) Henry

(b) coulomb

(c) watt

(d) watt-hour

2. Electric pressure is also called

(a) resistance

(b) power

(c) voltage

(d) energy

3. The substances which have a large number of free electrons and offer a low

resistance are called

(a) insulators

(b) inductors

(c) semi-conductors

(d) <u>conductors</u>

4. Out of the following which is not a poor conductor ?

(a) Cast iron

(b) <u>Copper</u>

(c) Carbon

(d) Tungsten

5. Out of the following which is an insulating material ?

(a) Copper

(b) Gold

(c) Silver

(d) <u>Paper</u>

6. The property of a conductor due to which it passes current is called

(a) resistance

(b) reluctance

(c) <u>conductance</u>

(d) inductance

7. Conductance is reciprocal of

(a) <u>resistance</u>

(b) inductance

(c) reluctance

(d) capacitance

8. The resistance of a conductor varies inversely as

(a) length

(b) <u>area of cross-section</u>

(c) temperature

(d) resistivity

9. With rise in temperature the resistance of pure metals

(a) <u>increases</u>

(b) decreases

(c) first increases and then decreases

(d) remains constant

10. With rise in temperature the resistance of semi-conductors

(a) decreases
(b) increases
(c) first increases and then decreases
(d) remains constant

11. The resistance of a copper wire 200 m long is 21 Q. If its thickness (diameter)
is 0.44 mm, its specific resistance is around
(a) 1.2 x 10~8 Q-m
(b) 1.4 x 10~8 Q-m
(c) 1.6 x 10""8 Q-m
(d) 1.8 x 10"8 Q-m

13. An instrument which detects electric current is known as
(a) voltmeter
(b) rheostat
(c) wattmeter
(d) galvanometer

14. In a circuit a 33 Q resistor carries a current of 2 A. The voltage across the resistor is
(a) 33 V
(b) 66 v
(c) 80 V
(d) 132 V

15. A light bulb draws 300 mA when the voltage across it is 240 V. The resistance of the light bulb is
(a) 400 Q
(b) 600 Q
(c) 800 Q
(d) 1000 Q

16. The resistance of a parallel circuit consisting of two branches is 12 ohms. If the resistance of one branch is 18 ohms, what is the resistance of the other ?
(a) 18 Q
(b) 36 Q
(c) 48 Q
(d) 64 Q

17. Four wires of same material, the same cross-sectional area and the same length when connected in parallel give a resistance of 0.25 Q. If the same four wires are connected is series the effective resistance will be

(a) 1 Q
(b) 2 Q
(c) 3 Q
(d) 4 Q

18. A current of 16 amperes divides between two branches in parallel of resistances 8 ohms and 12 ohms respectively. The current in each branch is
(a) 6.4 A, 6.9 A
(b) 6.4 A, 9.6 A
(c) 4.6 A, 6.9 A
(d) 4.6 A, 9.6 A

19. Current velocity through a copper conductor is
(a) the same as propagation velocity of electric energy
(b) independent of current strength
(c) of the order of a few ^.s/m
(d) nearly 3 x 108 m/s

20. Which of the following material has nearly zero temperature coefficient of resistance?
(a) Manganin
(b) Porcelain
(c) Carbon
(d) Copper

21. You have to replace 1500 Q resistor in radio. You have no 1500 Q resistor but have several 1000 Q ones which you would connect
(a) two in parallel
(b) two in parallel and one in series
(c) three in parallel
(d) three in series

22. Two resistors are said to be connected in series when
(a) same current passes in turn through both
(b) both carry the same value of current
(c) total current equals the sum of branch currents
(d) sum of IR drops equals the applied e.m.f.

23. Which of the following statement is true both for a series and a parallel D.C. circuit?
(a) Elements have individual currents
(b) Currents are additive
(c) Voltages are additive
(d) Power are additive

24. Which of the following materials has a negative temperature co-efficient of resistance?

(a) Copper
(b) Aluminum
(c) Carbon
(d) Brass

25. Ohm's law is not applicable to

(a) vacuum tubes
(b) carbon resistors
(c) high voltage circuits
(d) circuits with low current densities

26. Which is the best conductor of electricity ?

(a) Iron
(b) Silver
(c) Copper
(d) Carbon

27. For which of the following 'ampere second' could be the unit ?

(a) Reluctance
(b) Charge
(c) Power
(d) Energy

28. All of the following are equivalent to watt except

(a) (amperes) ohm
(b) joules/sec.
(c) amperes x volts
(d) amperes/volt

29. A resistance having rating 10 ohms, 10 W is likely to be a

(a) metallic resistor
(b) carbon resistor
(c) wire wound resistor
(d) variable resistor

30. Which one of the following does not have negative temperature co-efficient ?

(a) Aluminium
(b) Paper
(c) Rubber
(d) Mica

31. Varistors are

(a) insulators
(6) non-linear resistors
(c) carbon resistors
(d) resistors with zero temperature coefficient
32. Insulating materials have the function of
(a) preventing a short circuit between conducting wires
(b) preventing an open circuit between the voltage source and the load
(c) conducting very large currents
(d) storing very high currents
33. The rating of a fuse wire is always expressed in
(a) ampere-hours
(b) ampere-volts
(c) kWh
(d) amperes
34. The minimum charge on an ion is
(a) equal to the atomic number of the atom
(b) equal to the charge of an electron
(c) equal to the charge of the number of electrons in an atom (#) zero
35. In a series circuit with unequal resistances
(a) the highest resistance has the most of the current through it
(b) the lowest resistance has the highest voltage drop
(c) the lowest resistance has the highest current
(d) the highest resistance has the highest voltage drop
36. The filament of an electric bulb is made of
(a) carbon
(b) aluminium
(c) tungsten
(d) nickel
37. A 3 Q resistor having 2 A current will dissipate the power of
(a) 2 watts
(b) 4 watts
(c) 6 watts
(d) 8 watts
38. Which of the following statement is true?
(a) A galvanometer with low resistance in parallel is a voltmeter
(b) A galvanometer with high resistance in parallel is a voltmeter
(c) A galvanometer resistance in series is an ammeter with low
(d) A galvanometer with high resistance in series is an ammeter

39. The resistance of a few meters of wire conductor in closed electrical circuit is

(a) practically zero

(b) low

(c) high

(d) very high

40. If a parallel circuit is opened in the main line, the current

(a) increases in the branch of the lowest resistance

(b) increases in each branch

(c) is zero in all branches

(d) is zero in the highest resistive branch

41. If a wire conductor of 0.2 ohm resistance is doubled in length, its resistance becomes

(a) 0.4 ohm

(b) 0.6 ohm

(c) 0.8 ohm

(d) 1.0 ohm

42. Three 60 W bulbs are in parallel across the 60 V power line. If one bulb burns open

(a) there will be heavy current in the main line

(b) rest of the two bulbs will not light

(c) all three bulbs will light

(d) the other two bulbs will light

43. The four bulbs of 40 W each are connected in series swift a battery across them, which of the following statement is true ?

(a) The current through each bulb in same

(b) The voltage across each bulb is not same

(c) The power dissipation in each bulb is not same

(d) None of the above

44. Two resistances Rl and Ri are connected in series across the voltage source where Rl>Ri. The largest drop will be across

(a) Rl

(b) Ri

(c) either Rl or Ri

(d) none of them

46. A closed switch has a resistance of

(a) zero

(b) about 50 ohms

(c) about 500 ohms

(d) infinity

47. The hot resistance of the bulb's filament is higher than its cold resistance because the temperature co-efficient of the filament is

(a) zero

(b) negative

(c) positive

(d) about 2 ohms per degree

49. The insulation on a current carrying conductor is provided

(a) to prevent leakage of current

(b) to prevent shock

(c) both of above factors

(d) none of above factors

50. The thickness of insulation provided on the conductor depends on

(a) the magnitude of voltage on the conductor

(b) the magnitude of current flowing through it

(c) both (a) and (b)

(d) none of the above

51. Which of the following quantities remain the same in all parts of a series circuit ?

(a) Voltage

(b) Current

(c) Power

(d) Resistance

52. A 40 W bulb is connected in series with a room heater. If now 40 W bulb is replaced by 100 W bulb, the heater output will

(a) decrease

(b) increase

(c) remain same

(d) heater will burn out

53. In an electric kettle water boils in 10 m minutes. It is required to boil the boiler in 15 minutes, using same supply mains

(a) length of heating element should be decreased

(b) length of heating element should be increased

(c) length of heating element has no effect on heating if water

(d) none of the above

54. An electric filament bulb can be worked from

(a) D.C. supply only

(b) A.C. supply only

(c) Battery supply only

(d) All above

55. Resistance of a tungsten lamp as applied voltage increases

(a) decreases

(b) increases

(c) remains same

(d) none of the above

56. Electric current passing through the circuit produces

(a) magnetic effect

(b) luminous effect

(c) thermal effect

(d) chemical effect

(e) all above effects

57. Resistance of a material always decreases if

(a) temperature of material is decreased

(6) temperature of material is increased

(c) number of free electrons available become more

(d) none of the above is correct

58. If the efficiency of a machine is to be high, what should be low ?

(a) Input power

(b) Losses

(c) True component of power

(d) kWh consumed

(e) Ratio of output to input

59. When electric current passes through a metallic conductor, its temperature rises. This is due to

(a) collisions between conduction electrons and atoms

(b) the release of conduction electrons from parent atoms

(c) mutual collisions between metal atoms

(d) mutual collisions between conducting electrons

60. Two bulbs of 500 W and 200 W rated at 250 V will have resistance ratio as

(a) 4 : 25

(b) 25 : 4

(c) 2 : 5

(d) 5 : 2

61. A glass rod when rubbed with silk cloth is charged because

(a) it takes in proton

(b) its atoms are removed

(c) it gives away electrons

(d) it gives away positive charge

62. Whether circuit may be AC. or D.C. one, following is most effective in reducing the magnitude of the current.

(a) Reactor

(b) Capacitor

(c) Inductor

(d) Resistor

63. It becomes more difficult to remove

(a) any electron from the orbit

(6) first electron from the orbit

(c) second electron from the orbit

(d) third electron from the orbit

64. When one leg of parallel circuit is opened out the total current will

(a) reduce

(b) increase

(c) decrease

(d) become zero

65. In a lamp load when more than one lamp are switched on the total resistance of the load

(a) increases

(b) decreases

(c) remains same

(d) none of the above

66. Two lamps 100 W and 40 W are connected in series across 230 V (alternating).

Which of the following statement is correct ?

(a) 100 W lamp will glow brighter

(b) 40 W lamp will glow brighter

(c) Both lamps will glow equally bright

(d) 40 W lamp will fuse

67. Resistance of 220 V, 100 W lamp will be

(a) 4.84 Q

(b) 48.4 Q

(c) 484 ft

(d) 4840 Q

68. In the case of direct current

(a) magnitude and direction of current remains constant

(b) magnitude and direction of current changes with time

(c) magnitude of current changes with time

(d) magnitude of current remains constant

69. When electric current passes through a bucket full of water, lot of bubbling is

observed. This suggests that the type of supply is

(a) A.C.

(b) D.C.

(c) any of above two

(d) none of the above

70. Resistance of carbon filament lamp as the applied voltage increases.

(a) increases

(b) decreases

(c) remains same

(d) none of the above

71. Bulbs in street lighting are all connected in

(a) parallel

(b) series

(c) series-parallel

(d) end-to-end

72. For testing appliances, the wattage of test lamp should be

(a) very low

(b) low

(c) high

(d) any value

73. Switching of a lamp in house produces noise in the radio. This is because switching operation produces

(a) arcs across separating contacts

(b) mechanical noise of high intensity

(c) both mechanical noise and arc between contacts

(d) none of the above

74. Sparking occurs when a load is switched off because the circuit has high

(a) resistance

(b) inductance
(c) capacitance
(d) impedance

75. Copper wire of certain length and resistance is drawn out to three times its
length without change in volume, the new resistance of wire becomes
(a) 1/9 times
(b) 3 times
(c) 9 times
(d) unchanged

76. When resistance element of a heater fuses and then we reconnect it after removing a portion of it, the power of the heater will
(a) decrease
(b) increase
(c) remain constant
(d) none of the above

77. A field of force can exist only between
(a) two molecules
(b) two ions
(c) two atoms
(d) two metal particles

78. A substance whose molecules consist of dissimilar atoms is called
(a) semi-conductor
(b) super-conducto
(c) compound
(d) insulator

79. International ohm is defined in terms of the resistance of
(a) a column of mercury
(b) a cube of carbon
(c) a cube of copper
(d) the unit length of wire

80. Three identical resistors are first connected in parallel and then in series.
The resultant resistance of the first combination to the second will be
(a) 9 times
(b) 1/9 times
(c) 1/3 times
(d) 3 times

91. Which method can be used for absolute measurement of resistances ?

(a) Lorentz method

(b) Releigh method

(c) Ohm's law method

(d) Wheatstone bridge method

92. Three 6 ohm resistors are connected to form a triangle. What is the resistance between any two corners ?

(a) 3/2 Q

(b 6 Q

(c) 4 Q

(d) 8/3 Q

93. Ohm's law is not applicable to

(a) semi-conductors

(b) D.C. circuits

(c) small resistors

(d) high currents

94. Two copper conductors have equal length. The cross-sectional area of one conductor is four times that of the other. If the conductor having smaller crosssectional area has a resistance of 40 ohms the resistance of other conductor will be

(a) 160 ohms

(b) 80 ohms

(c) 20 ohms

(d) 10 ohms

95. A nichrome wire used as a heater coil has the resistance of 2 £2/m. For a heater of 1 kW at 200 V, the length of wire required will be

(a) 80 m

(b) 60 m

(c) 40 m

(d) 20 m

96. Temperature co-efficient of resistance is expressed in terms of

(a) ohms/°C

(b) mhos/ohm°C

(c) ohms/ohm°C

98. When current flows through heater coil it glows but supply wiring does not glow because

(a) current through supply line flows at slower speed

(b) supply wiring is covered with insulation layer

(c) resistance of heater coil is more than the supply wires

(d) supply wires are made of superior material

99. The condition for the validity under Ohm's law is that

(a) resistance must be uniform

(b) current should be proportional to the size of the resistance

(c) resistance must be wire wound type

(d) temperature at positive end should be more than the temperature at negative end

100. Which of the following statement is correct ?

(a) A semi-conductor is a material whose conductivity is same as between that of a conductor and an insulator

(b) A semi-conductor is a material which has conductivity having average value of conductivity of metal and insulator

(c) A semi-conductor is one which con¬ducts only half of the applied voltage

(d) A semi-conductor is a material made of alternate layers of conducting material and insulator

101. A rheostat differs from potentiometer in the respect that it

(a) has lower wattage rating

(b) has higher wattage rating

(c) has large number of turns

(d) offers large number of tapping

102. The weight of an aluminium conductor as compared to a copper conductor of identical cross-section, for the same electrical resistance, is

(a) 50%

(b) 60%

(c) 100%

(d) 150%

103. An open resistor, when checked with an ohm-meter reads

(a) zero

(b) infinite

(c) high but within tolerance

(d) low but not zero

104. are the materials having electrical conductivity much less than most of the metals but much greater than that of typical insulators.

(a) Varistors

(b) Thermistor

(c) Semi-conductors
(d) Variable resistors
105. All good conductors have high
(a) conductance
(b) resistance
(c) reluctance
(d) thermal conductivity
106. Voltage dependent resistors are usually made from
(a) charcoal
(b) silicon carbide
(c) nichrome
(d) graphite
107. Voltage dependent resistors are used
(a) for inductive circuits
(b) to supress surges
(c) as heating elements
(d) as current stabilizers
108. The ratio of mass of proton to that of electron is nearly
(a) 1840
(b) 1840
(c) 30
(d) 4
109. The number of electrons in the outer most orbit of carbon atom is
(a) 3
(b) 4
(c) 6
(d) 7
110. With three resistances connected in parallel, if each dissipates 20 W the total power supplied by the voltage source equals
(a) 10 W
(b) 20 W
(c) 40 W
(d) 60 W
111. A thermistor has
(a) positive temperature coefficient
(b) negative temperature coefficient
(c) zero temperature coefficient
(d) variable temperature coefficient

112. If/, R and t are the current, resistance and time respectively, then according

to Joule's law heat produced will be proportional to

(a) I2Rt

(b) I2Rf

(c) I2R2t

(d) I2R2t*

113. Nichrome wire is an alloy of

(a) lead and zinc

(b) chromium and vanadium

(c) nickel and chromium

(d) copper and silver

114. When a voltage of one volt is applied, a circuit allows one micro ampere current to flow through it. The conductance of the circuit is

(a) 1 n-mho

(b) 106 mho

(c) 1 milli-mho

(d) none of the above

115. Which of the following can have negative temperature coefficient ?

(a) Compounds of silver

(6) Liquid metals

(c) Metallic alloys

(d) Electrolytes

116. Conductance : mho ::

(a) resistance : ohm

(b) capacitance : henry

(c) inductance : farad

(d) lumen : steradian

117. 1 angstrom is equal to

(a) 10-8 mm

(b) 10"6 cm

(c) 10"10 m

(d) 10~14 m

118. One newton meter is same as

(a) one watt

(b) one joule

(c) five joules

(d) one joule second

1. The insulating material for a cable should have
(a) low cost
(b) high dielectric strength
(c) high mechanical strength
(d) all of the above
2. Which of the following protects a cable against mechanical injury ?
(a) Bedding
(b) Sheath
(c) Armouring
(d) None of the above
3. Which of the following insulation is used in cables ?
(a) Varnished cambric
(b) Rubber
(c) Paper
(d) Any of the above
4. Empire tape is
(a) varnished cambric
(b) vulcanised rubber
(c) impregnated paper
(d) none of the above
5. The thickness of the layer of insulation on the conductor, in cables, depends upon
(a) reactive power
(b) power factor
(c) voltage
(d) current carrying capacity
6. The bedding on a cable consists of
(a) hessian cloth
(b) jute
(c) any of the above
(d) none of the above
7. The insulating material for cables should
(a) be acid proof
(b) be non-inflammable
(c) be non-hygroscopic
(d) have all above properties
8. In a cable immediately above metallic sheath ______ is provided.
(a) earthing connection

(b) bedding

(c) armouring

(d) none of the above

9. The current carrying capacity of cables in D.C. is more thanthat in A.C. mainly due to

(a) absence of harmonics

(b) non-existence of any stability limit

(c) smaller dielectric loss

(d) absence of ripples

(e) none of the above

10. In case of three core flexible cable the colour of the neutral is

(a) blue

(b) black

(c) brown

(d) none of the above

11 cables are used for 132 kV lines.

(a) High tension

(b) Super tension

(c) Extra high tension

(d) Extra super voltage

12. Conduit pipes are normally used to protect ______ cables.

(a) unsheathed cables

(b) armoured

(c) PVC sheathed cables

(d) all of the above

13. The minimum dielectric stress in a cable is at

(a) armour

(b) bedding

(c) conductor surface

(d) lead sheath

14. In single core cables armouring is not done to

(a) avoid excessive sheath losses

(b) make it flexible

(c) either of the above

(d) none of the above

15. Dielectric strength of rubber is around

(a) 5 kV/mm

(b) 15 kV/mm

(c) 30 kV/mm
(d) 200 kV/mm
16. Low tension cables are generally used up to
(a) 200 V
(b) 500 V
(c) 700 V
(d) 1000 V
17. In a cable, the maximum stress under operating conditions is at
(a) insulation layer
(b) sheath
(c) armour
(d) conductor surface
18. High tension cables are generally used up to
(a) 11kV
(b) 33kV
(c) 66 kV
(d) 132 kV
19. The surge resistance of cable is
(a) 5 ohms
(b) 20 ohms
(c) 50 ohms
(d) 100 ohms
20. PVC stands for
(a) polyvinyl chloride
(b) post varnish conductor
(c) pressed and varnished cloth
(d) positive voltage conductor
21. In the cables, the location of fault is usually found out by comparing
(a) the resistance of the conductor
(b) the inductance of conductors
(c) the capacitances of insulated conductors
(d) all above parameters
22. In capacitance grading of cables we use a _______ dielectric.
(a) composite
(b) porous
(c) homogeneous
(d) hygroscopic
23. Pressure cables are generally not used beyond

(a) 11 kV
(b) 33 kV
(c) 66 kV
(d) 132 kV

24. The material for armouring on cable is usually
(a) steel tape
(b) galvanised steel wire
(c) any of the above
(d) none of the above

25. Cables, generally used beyond 66 kV are
(a) oil filled
(b) S.L. type
(c) belted
(d) armoured

26. The relative permittivity of rubber is
(a) between 2 and 3
(b) between 5 and 6
(c) between 8 and 10
(d) between 12 and 14

27. Solid type cables are considered unreliable beyond 66 kV because
(a) insulation may melt due to higher temperature
(b) skin effect dominates on the conductor
(c) of corona loss between conductor and sheath material
(d) there is a danger of breakdown of insulation due to the presence of voids

28. If the length of a cable is doubled, its capacitance
(a) becomes one-fourth
(b) becomes one-half
(c) becomes double
(d) remains unchanged

29. In cables the charging current
(a) lags the voltage by 90°
(b) leads the voltage by 90°
(c) lags the voltage by 180°
(d) leads the voltage by 180°

30. A certain cable has an insulation of relative permittivity 4. If the insulation is

replaced by one of relative permittivity 2, the capacitance of the cable will become

(a) one half

(6) double

(c) four times

(d) none of the above

31. If a cable of homogeneous insulation has a maximum stress of 10 kV/ mm,

then the dielectric strength of insulation should be

(a) 5 kV/mm

(b) 10 kV/mm

(c) 15 kV/mm

(d) 30 kV/mm

32. In the cables, sheaths are used to

(a) prevent the moisture from entering the cable

(b) provide enough strength

(e) provide proper insulation

(d) none of the above

33. The intersheaths in the cables are used to

(a) minimize the stress

(b) avoid the requirement of good insulation

(c) provide proper stress distribution

(d) none of the above

34. The electrostatic stress in underground cables is

(a) same at the conductor and the sheath

(b) minimum at the conductor and maximum at the sheath

(c) maximum at the conductor and minimum at the sheath

(d) zero at the conductor as well as on the sheath

(e) none of the above

35. The breakdown of insulation of the cable can be avoided economically by the

use of

(a) inter-sheaths

(b) insulating materials with different dielectric constants

(c) both (a) and (b)

(d) none of the above

36. The insulation of the cable decreases with

(a) the increase in length of the insulation

(b) the decrease in the length of the insulation
(c) either (a) or (b)
(d) none of the above
37. A cable carrying alternating current has
(a) hysteresis losses only
(b) hysteresis and leakage losses only
(c) hysteresis, leakage and copper losses only
(d) hysteresis, leakage, copper and friction losses
38. In a cable the voltage stress is maximum at
(a) sheath
(6) insulator
(e) surface of the conductor
(d) core of the conductor
39. Capacitance grading of cable implies
(a) use of dielectrics of different permeabilities
(b) grading according to capacitance of cables per km length
(c) cables using single dielectric in different concentrations
(d) capacitance required to be introduced at different lengths to counter the effect
of inductance
40. Underground cables are laid at sufficient depth
(a) to minimise temperature stresses
(b) to avoid being unearthed easily due to removal of soil
(c) to minimise the effect of shocks and vibrations due to gassing vehicles, etc.
(d) for all of the above reasons
41. The advantage of cables over overhead transmission lines is
(a) easy maintenance
(b) low cost
(c) can be used in congested areas
(d) can be used in high voltage circuits
42. The thickness of metallic shielding on cables is usually
(a) 0.04 mm
(b) 0.2 to 0.4 mm
(e) 3 to 5 mm
(d) 40 to 60 mm
43. Cables for 220 kV lines are invariably
(a) mica insulated

(b) paper insulated
(c) compressed oil or compressed gas insulated
(d) rubber insulated
(e) none of the above

44. Is a cable is to be designed for use on 1000 kV, which insulation would you prefer ?
(a) Polyvinyle chloride
(b) Vulcanised rubber
(c) Impregnated paper
(d) Compressed SFe gas

45. If a power cable and a communication cable are to run parallel the minimum
distance between the two, to avoid interference, should be
(a) 2 cm
(b) 10 cm
(c) 50 cm
(d) 400 cm

46. Copper as conductor for cables is used as
(a) annealed
(b) hardened and tempered
(c) hard drawn
(d) alloy with chromium

47. The insulating material should have
(a) low permittivity
(b) high resistivity
(c) high dielectric strength
(d) all of the above

48. The advantage of oil filled cables is
(a) more perfect impregnation
(b) smaller overall size
(c) no ionisation, oxidation and formation of voids
(d) all of the above

49. The disadvantage with paper as insulating material is
(a) it is hygroscopic
(6) it has high capacitance
(c) it is an organic material
(d) none of the above

50. The breakdown voltage of a cable depends on

(a) presence of moisture

(b) working temperature

(c) time of application of the voltage

(d) all of the above

1. “The mass of an ion liberated at an electrode is directly proportional to the quantity of electricity”.

The above statement is associated with

(a) Newton’s law

(b) Faraday’s law of electromagnetic

(c) Faraday’s law of electrolysis

(d) Gauss’s law

2. The charge required to liberate one gram equivalent of any substance is known as _______ constant

(a) time

(b) Faraday’s

(c) Boltzman

3. During the charging of a lead-acid cell

(a) its voltage increases

(b) it gives out energy

(c) its cathode becomes dark chocolate brown in colour

(d) specific gravity of H2SO4 decreases

4. The capacity of a lead-acid cell does not depend on its

(a) temperature

(b) rate of charge

(c) rate of discharge

(d) quantity of active material

5. During charging the specific gravity of the electrolyte of a lead-acid battery

(a) increases

(b) decreases

(c) remains the same

(d) becomes zero

6. The active materials on the positive and negative plates of a fully charged leadacid battery are

(a) lead and lead peroxide

(b) lead sulphate and lead

(c) lead peroxide and lead

(d) none of the above

7. When a lead-acid battery is in fully charged condition, the colour of its positive
plate is
(a) dark grey
(b) brown
(c) dark brown
(d) none of above
8. The active materials of a nickel-iron battery are
(a) nickel hydroxide
(6) powdered iron and its oxide
(c) 21% solution of KOH
(d) all of the above
9. The ratio of ampere-hour efficiency to watt-hour efficiency of a lead-acid cell is
(a) just one
(b) always greater than one
(c) always less than one
(d) none of the above.
10. The best indication about the state of charge on a lead-acid battery is given by
(a) output voltage
(b) temperature of electrolyte
(c) specific gravity of electrolyte
(d) none of the above
11. The storage battery generally used in electric power station is
(a) nickel-cadmium battery
(b) zinc-carbon battery
(c) lead-acid battery
(d) none of the above
12. The output voltage of a charger is
(a) less than the battery voltage
(b) higher than the battery voltage
(c) the same as the battery voltage
(d) none of the above
13. Cells are connected in series in order to
(a) increase the voltage rating
(6) increase the current rating
(c) increase the life of the cells

(d) none of the above

14. Five 2 V cells are connected in parallel. The output voltage is

(a) 1 V

(6) 1.5 V

(c) 1.75 V

(d) 2 V

15. The capacity of a battery is expressed in terms of

(a) current rating

(b) voltage rating

(c) ampere-hour rating

(d) none of the above

16. Duringthe charging and discharging of a nickel-iron cell

(a) corrosive fumes are produced

(b) water is neither formed nor absorbed

(c) nickel hydroxide remains unsplit

(d) its e.m.f. remains constant

17. As compared to constant-current system, the constant-voltage system of charging a lead acid cell has the advantage of

(a) reducing time of charging

(b) increasing cell capacity

(c) both (a) and (b)

(d) avoiding excessive gassing

18. A dead storage battery can be revived by

(a) adding distilled water

(6) adding so-called battery restorer

(c) a dose of H2SO4

(d) none of the above

19. As compared to a lead-acid cell, the efficiency of a nickel-iron cell is less due to its

(a) compactness

(b) lower e.m.f.

(c) small quantity of electrolyte used

(d) higher internal resistance

20. Trickle charging of a storage battery helps to

(a) maintain proper electrolyte level

(b) increase its reserve capacity

(c) prevent sulphation

(d) keep it fresh and fully charged

21. Those substances of the cell which take active part in chemical combination and hence produce electricity during charging or discharging are known as_______materials.

(a) passive
(b) active
(c) redundant
(d) inert

22. In a lead-acid cell dilute sulphuric acid (electrolyte) approximately comprises the following

(a) one part H2O, three parts H2SO4
(b) two parts H2O, two parts H2SO4
(c) three parts H2O, one part H2SO4
(d) all H2S04

23. It is noticed that durum charging

(a) there is a rise in voltage
(b) energy is absorbed by the cell
(c) specific gravity of H2SO4 is increased
(d) all of the above

24. It is noticed that during discharging the following does not happen

(a) both anode and cathode become PbS04
(b) specific gravity of H2SO4 decreases
(c) voltage of the cell decreases
(d) the cell absorbs energy

25. The ampere-hour efficiency of a leadacid cell is normally between

(a) 20 to 30%
(b) 40 to 50%
(c) 60 to 70%
(d) 90 to 95%

26. The watt-hour efficiency of a lead-acid cell varies between

(a) 25 to 35%
(b) 40 to 60%
(c) 70 to 80%
(d) 90 to 95%

27. The capacity of a lead-acid cell is measured in

(a) amperes
(b) ampere-hours
(c) watts
(d) watt-hours

28. The capacity of a lead-acid cell depends on
(a) rate of discharge
(b) temperature
(c) density of electrolyte
(d) all above

29. When the lead-acid cell is fully charged, the electrolyte assumes ______appearance
(a) dull
(b) reddish
(c) bright
(d) milky

30. The e.m.f. of an Edison cell, when fully charged, is nearly
(a) 1.4 V
(b) 1 V
(c) 0.9 V
(d) 0.8 V

31. The internal resistance of an alkali cell is nearly ______ times that of the leadacid cell.
(a) two
(b) three
(c) four
(d) five

32. The average charging voltage for alkali cell is about
(a) 1 V
(b) 1.2 V
(c) 1.7 V
(d) 2.1 V

33. On the average the ampere-hour efficiency of an Edison cell is about
(a) 40%
(b) 60%
(c) 70%
(d) 80%

34. The active material of the positive plates of silver-zinc batteries is
(a) silver oxide
(b) lead oxide
(c) lead
(d) zinc powder

35. Lead-acid cell has a life of nearly charges and discharges

(a) 500

(b) 700

(c) 1000

(d) 1250

36. Life of the Edison cell is at least

(a) five years

(b) seven years

(c) eight years

(d) ten years

37. The internal resistance of a lead-acid cell is that of Edison cell

(a) less than

(b) more than

(c) equal to

(d) none of the above

38. Electrolyte used in an Edison cell is

(a) NaOH

(b) KOH

(c) HC1

(d) HN03

39. Electrolyte used in a lead-acid cell is

(a) NaOH

(b) onlyH2S04

(c) only water

(d) dilute H2SO4

40. Negative plate of an Edison cell is made of

(a) copper

(b) lead

(c) iron

(d) silver oxide

41. The open circuit voltage of any storage cell depends wholly upon

(a) its chemical constituents

(b) on the strength of its electrolyte

(c) its temperature

(d) all above

42. The specific gravity of electrolyte is measured by

(a) manometer

(6) a mechanical gauge

(c) hydrometer

(d) psychrometer

43. When the specific gravity of the electrolyte of a lead-acid cell is reduced to 1.1 to 1.15 the cell is in

(a) charged state

(b) discharged state

(c) both (a) and (b)

(d) active state

44. In _______ system the charging current is intermittently controlled at either a

maximum or minimum value

(a) two rate charge control

(b) trickle charge

(c) floating charge

(d) an equalizing charge

45. Over charging

(a) produces excessive gassing

(b) loosens the active material

(e) increases the temperature resulting in buckling of plates

(d) all above

46. Undercharging

(a) reduces specific gravity of the electrolyte

(b) increases specific gravity of the electrolyte

(c) produces excessive gassing

(d) increases the temperature

47. Internal short circuits are caused by

(a) breakdown of one or more separators

(b) excess accumulation of sediment at the bottom of the cell

(c) both (a) and (b)

(d) none of the above

48. The effect of sulphation is that the internal resistance

(a) increases

(b) decreases

(c) remains same

(d) none of the above

49. Excessive formation of lead sulphate on the surface of the plates happens because of

(a) allowing a battery to stand in discharged condition for a long time

(b) topping up with electrolyte

(c) persistent undercharging

(d) all above

50. The substances which combine together to store electrical energy during the charge are called _______ materials

(a) active

(b) passive

(c) inert

(d) dielectric

85] A heater draws a current of 8A when connected to a 240V source] What is the resistance value of the heater element in ohms?

A] 40

B] 20

C] 30

D] 60

86] An electric soldering iron with an 80 ohms heating element is plugged into a 240V outlet] How much current will be drawn by the iron?

A] 2A

B] 3A

C] 4A

D] 5A

87] The alternator in a car delivers 4A and has a load of 3 ohms connected across its terminals] Find the voltage of the circuit

A] 18V

B] 24V

C] 12V

D] 16V

88] Three resistors of 1K ohms, 2K ohms and 7K ohms are connected in series with a 30 V supply] If 2 K ohms and 7 K ohms resistors are open circuited, a voltmeter connected across the 7K ohms resistor will indicate...

A] 10 k ohms, 3A

B] 10 k ohms, 300mA

C] 10 k ohms, 3 mA

D] 5 k ohms, 6 mA

89] A voltage source produces an IR drop of 40V across a 20 ohms resistance, 60V across a 30 ohms resistance and 180V across a 90 ohms resistance all in series] How much is the applied voltage?

A] 180 V

B] 240 V

C] 100 V

D] <u>280 V</u>

90] Three resistors 27 ohms, 47 ohms and 68 ohms are connected in parallel] What is the otal resistance?

A] <u>less than 27 ohms</u>

B] greater than 68 ohms

C] between 27 and 47 ohms

D] sum of all the three resistances

91] One million and one mege ohms resistors are there if connected both in parallel, what would be the combined resistance value?

A] <u>0.5 mega ohm</u>

B] 0.5 milli ohm

C] 0.5 kilo ohm

D] 0.5 ohm

92] A 24 ohms and a 8 ohms resistors in parallel gets a combined resistance of...

A] <u>6 ohms</u>

B] 12 ohms

C] 3 ohms

D] 32 ohms

93] Resistors of the following values are connected in parallel, 5 ohms, 5 kilo-ohms, 50 kilo-ohms, 5 mega ohms] Their equivalent resistance will be very near to...

A] <u>4.5 ohms</u>

B] 4500 ohms

C] 45000 ohms

D] 4,500,000 ohms

94] The resistance of given wire is 2 ohms] The resistance of the other wire made of the same material having twice the length and twice the cross sectional area is...

A] 5 ohms

B] 6 ohms

C] <u>2 ohms</u>

D] 8 ohms

95] If the area of a metal wire of a given length is doubles, its resistance will...

A] be doubled

B] <u>be halved</u>

C] remain the same

D] be four times more

96].Among the following only one is regarded as resistance wire

A] gold

B] silver

C] nichrome

D] copper

97] Arc heating occurs when the air between electrodes of opposite polarity becomes..

A] moistened

B] dry

C] ionized

D] none of the above

98] The meter used to measure the temperature of furnace is...

A] hydrometer

B] pyrometer

C] hygrometer

D] tachometer

99] in the case of electrolyte a rise in temperature causes...

A] decrease in resistance

B] increase in resistance

C] no change in resistance

D] none of the above

100] Heat developed in a conductor is proportional to the...

A] square of the power

B] square of the resistance

C] square of the current

D] square of the time

101] Out of the four metal/alloys given below, one has almost no change in resistance for temperature change...

A] nickel

B] nichrome

C] platinum

D] manganin

102] A material that is slightly repelled by a magnet is called ...

A] magnetic

B] paramagnetic

C] diamagnetic

D] ferromagnetic

103] A material that can be magnetized only very slightly is called...

A] magnetic

B] paramagnetic

C] diamagnetic

D] ferromagnetic

104] Substances that can be magnetized easily and make very strong magnets are called...

A] ferromagnetic

B] diamagnetic

C] paramagnetic

D] permanent magnetic

105] A substance that has a high retentivity can be used for the manufacture of...

A] electromagnets

B] permanent magnets

C] temporary magnets

D] paramagnets

106] A substance that has low retentivity can be used for the manufacture of...

A] electromagnets

B] permanent magnets

C] bar magnets

D] paramagnets

107] The symbol for inductance is...

A] H

B] I

C] L

D] X

108] Tube lamp choke is the best example of...

A] open circuited

B] short circuited

C] grounded

D] connected to the neutral line

109] The initial function of a choke in a tube light circuit is to...

A] limit the starting current

B] induce high voltage

C] heat up the filament

D] limit the current after starting

110] The second function of a choke in a tube light circuit is to...

A] limit the starting current

B] induce high voltage

C] heat up the filament

D] limit the current after starting

111] The periodic time of a wave from is 2ms] Calculate the frequency

A] 50 HZ

B] 5 HZ

C] 500HZ

D] 5 KHZ

112] How big is the peak amplitude of a sine-wave with an effective value of 220 volts?

A] 311 V

B] 380 V

C] 400 V

D] 440 V

113] The peak-to-peak voltage is 99V] how big is the effective value of the sine wave?

A] 70 V

B] 44.5V

C] 49.5 V

D] 35 V

114] A moving coil voltmeter reads 10 V AC] How big is the effective voltage?

A] higher

B] lower

C] the same

D] 10% higher

115] A moving iron ammeter reads 10 A] how big is the peak current of the oscillation?

A] 7.07 A

B] 1.1414A

C] 70.7 A

D] 14.1 A

116] A current of 2 amps flows through a resistance of 10 ohms] The power dissipated in the resistance is equal to...

A] 20 watts

B] 200 watts

C] 40 watts

D] 5 watts

117] If the frequency changes from 50 HZ to 100 HZ keeping voltage constant, the inductive reactance of coil connected to supply...

A] remains same

B] become half

C] become doubled

D] become 4 times

118] Capacitance is not affected by...

A] plate area

B] distance between plates

C] dialectic material

D] frequency

119] The capacitive reactance of a capacitor varies...

A] directly with frequency

B] inversely with frequency

C] directly with applied voltage

D] inversely with applied voltage

120] A capacitor acquired 3 coulombs of charge when 6 volts are applied across it] It has a capacitance of ...

A] 0.5 farad

B] 3 farads

C] 3 farads

D] 18 farads

121] A capacitor is connected across a 200 volt AC line, its minimum voltage rating should be...

A] 100 volts

B] 200 Volts

C] 300 volts

D] 400 volts

122] when testing a capacitor with an ohmmeter, the meter indicates some resistance] The capacitor under test is...

A] leaky

B] open

C] good

D] short

123] The total capacitance of a 40 micro farad capacitor connected in series with an 80 micro farad capacitor is...

A] 26.7 micro farad

B] 40 micro farad

C] 60.6 micro farad

D] 120 micro farad

124] For obtaining 1 micro farad capacitor from 3 nos] of 3 micro farad capacitors we have to connect...

A] all in parallel

B] all in series

C] 2 series and one in parallel

D] none of the above

125] In an AC series circuit having R and C the current flowing through the capacitor will be...

A] lagging the voltage

B] leading the voltage

C] in phase with the voltage

D] none of the above

126] If the frequency of the supply is increased in the R-C series circuit the capacitive reactance will be

A] reduced

B] increased

C] having no effect

D] none of the above

127] Power companies are interested in improving the power factor to

A] reduce line current

B] increase motor efficiency

C] increase volt-amperes

D] decrease power

128] A capacitor increases the power factor value of an AC motor load when it is connected...

A] in series with the motor

B] in series with the starter

C] in parallel with the motor

D] in series with the main winding

129] Normally, the power factor of an incandescent lighting circuit is..

A] 0

B] 0.5

C] 0.707

D] 1.0

130] When resistance alone is used to determine current in an RLC series circuit, the circuit is...

A] an inductive circuit

B] a capacitive circuit

C] a combination circuit

D] a resonant circuit

131] Inductive reactance is directly related to..

A] resistance

B] frequency

C] capacitance

D] power

132] Synchronous motor when used for power factor improvement should be...

A] under excited

B] over excited

C] loaded

D] running at no load

133] In a RL parallel circuit, the opposition to total current is called...

A] reactance

B] resistance

C] a vector sum

D] impedance

134] In a AC parallel RL circuit, the power dissipated at the

A] impedance

B] resistance

C] inductance

D] capacitance

135] How much is the nominal output voltage of a carbon zinc cell?

A] 12V

B] 1.5V

C] 2.0V

D] 2.2V

136] Cells are connected in series to..

A] increase the output voltage

B] decreases the output voltage

C] decrease the internal resistance

D] increase the current capacity

54137connected in

A] series

B] parallel

C] series-parallel

D] parallel-series

138] The capacity of a cell is measured in

A] watt-hour

B] watts

C] amperes

D] ampere-hour

139] The primary cell which has the shortest shelf life is

A] carbon – zinc

B] alkaline

C] mercury

D] lithium

140] The cell which has very high energy density for given weight or volume to

A] carbon-zinc

B] alkaline

C] mercury

D] lithium

141] A 100-Ah capacity battery should deliver a current of 8A for approximately...

A] 12 h

B] 8 h

C] 20 h

D] 100 h

142] When the battery is needed to be kept idle for a long time...

A] overcharge the battery

B] remove electrolyte

C] clean the plates with distilled water

D] dry them and store the battery in cool dry clean place

143] The active materials of the nickel iron cell are...

A] nickel hydroxide

B] powdered iron and its oxide

C] 21% solution of caustic potash

D] all the above materials

144] The capacity of a cell is measured in

A] watt hour

B] watts

C] amperes

D] ampere-hour

145] To charge a secondary cell, the system used is

A] low voltage AC

B] high voltage AC

C] AC

D] DC

146] What is the number of phases in a normal industrial supply system?

A] one

B] three

C] four

D] two

147] In a 3 phase star connected alternator, the coils have a phase difference of...

A] 120◦

B] 240◦

C] 60◦

D] 360◦

148] Delta connection is used no one of the following

A] primary of the transmission line transformer

B] alternator winding

C] secondary of the distribution transformer

D] primary of the distribution transformer

149] Which method can be used to measure the power in a 3-phase unbalanced load system?

A] one wattmeter method

B] tow wattmeter method

C] three wattmeter method

D] three ammeter method

150] Two wattmeters can be used to measure 3-hase power in a 3-phase, 3 wire system with...

A] balanced load

B] unbalanced load

C] balanced as well as unbalanced load

D] out of balanced load

151] A single wattmeter can be used to measure power in a 3-phase system only when the load is..

A] balanaced

B] unbalanced

C] balanced as well as unbalanced load

D] constant

152] The force producing movement of the pointer in an indicating instrument is called as...

A] deflecting force

B] controlling force

C] damping force

D] distracting force

153] A permanent magnet moving coil instrument will read...

A] only AC quantities

B] only DC quantities

C] both AC and DC quantities

D] pulsating quantities

154] An instrument using gravity control will read correctly if used in..

A] vertical position only

B] horizontal position only

C] inclined position only

D] any position

155] Which one of the following damping methods is used in permanent magnet moving coil instrument?

A] air damping

B] fluid damping

C] spring damping

D] eddy current damping

156] Moving coil instrument works on the effect of...

A] chemical effect

B] heating effect

C] electrostatic effect

D] electromagnetic effect

157] The meter installed at your house to measure electrical energy is an example of...

A] indication type instrument

B] recording type instrument

C] indicating as well as recording type instrument

D] integrating type instrument

158].Which of the following material is preferred for permanent magnet?

A] alnico

B] y-alloy

C] silicon steel

D] wrought iron

159] The instrument which could be classified as absolute instrument is...

A] milli ammeter

B] micro ammeter

C] galvanometer

D] tangent galvanomer

160] Which of the following methods of damping is commonly used in moving iron instrument?

A] Air damping

B] fluid damping

C] eddy current damping

D] viscosity damping

161] The deflecting torque of a moving iron instrument is directly proportional to the..

A] current

B] square of the current

C] square root of the current

D] voltage

162]Which of the following is used for measuring the medium resistance directly?

A] ammeter

B] megger

C] ohmmeter

D] voltmeter

163] An ohmmeter is used for measuring the...

A] insulation resistance

B] resistance

C] current

D] potential difference

164] Which of the following components is not a part of an ohmmeter?

A] fixed resistor

B] variable resistor

C] capacitor

D] battery

165] In shunt ohmmeter, maximum deflection signifies ..

A] maximum resistance

B] minimum resistance

C] a fault in the megger

D] none of these

166].An unknown DC voltage is to be measured, which measuring range will you select first?

A] 500V

B] 50V

C] 1.5 V

D] 0.5V

167].An unknown direct current of micro ampere rating is to be measured, which measuring range will you select first?

A] 20 micro amp

B] 15 micro amp

C] 150 micro amp

D] 500 micro amp

168] A multimeter cannot measure...

A] current

B] potential difference

C] capacitance

D] resistance

169] Dynamometer type meters are used to measure...

A] only AC quantities

B] only DC quantities

C] both AC and DC

D] pulsating AC only

170] Which effect is used in wattmeter?

A] electrodynamic effect

B] thermal effect

C] chemical effect

D] electrostatic effect

171] Which of the instrument listed below operates efficiently as wattmeter in both AC and DC?

A] PMMC instrument

B] <u>dynamometer instrument</u>

C] hot wire instrument

D] MI instrument

172] Electrodynamic type of instrument are used commonly for the measurement of...

A] voltage

B] current

C] resistance D]

173] When the phase and neutral of the energy meter are interchanged, its disc...

A] <u>rotates in reverse direction</u>

B] rotates in correct direction

C] will stop

D] rotates slowly

E] rotates at high speed

174] When the disc of energy meter is rotating even without connecting any load, the error is called

A] <u>creeping error</u>

B] phase error

C] friction error

D] temperature error

175] AC single phase energy meters record the energy in the unit of...

A] <u>kilowatt hours</u>

B] number of thousands of disc rotation

C] volt amperes

D] kilo volt ampere

176] A megger measures resistance in...

A] ohms

B] hundreds of ohms

C] thousands of ohms

D] <u>millions of ohms</u>

177] A megger is exclusively designed for measuring..

A] <u>very high resistance</u>

B] very low resistance

C] ground faults in power lines

D] over loads on DC motors

178] For pipe earthing the minimum internal diameter of galvanized iron of steel pipe required is...

A] 12.5 mm
B] 16mm
C] 3.5 mm
D] 4 m
179] The earth conductor provides a path to ground for..
A] leakage current
B] over current
C] high voltage
D] circuit current
180] if the size of the circuit copper conductor is 10 sq-mm then the size of earth conductor in G.I] wire should be...
A] 1.5 sq.mm
B] 2.5 sq.mm
C] 5 sq.mm
D] 10 sq.mm
181] One calory is equal to,,,
A] 4187 joules
B] 418.7 joules
C] 41.87 joules
D] 4.187 joules
1. Tesla is a unit of
(a) field strength
(b) inductance
(c) flux density
(d) flux
2. A permeable substance is one
(a) which is a good conductor
(6) which is a bad conductor
(c) which is a strong magnet
(d) through which the magnetic lines of force can pass very easily
3. The materials having low retentivity are suitable for making
(a) weak magnets
(b) temporary magnets
(c) permanent magnets
(d) none of the above
4. A magnetic field exists around
(a) iron
(b) copper

(c) aluminium

(d) moving charges

5. Ferrites are materials.

(a) paramagnetic

(b) diamagnetic

(c) ferromagnetic

(d) none of the above

6. Air gap has________eluctance as compared to iron or steel path

(a) little

(b) lower

(c) higher

(d) zero

7. The direction of magnetic lines of force is

(a) from south pole to north pole

(b) from north pole to south pole

(c) from one end of the magnet to another

(d) none of the above

8. Which of the following is a vector quantity ?

(a) Relative permeability

(b) Magnetic field intensity

(c) Flux density

(d) Magnetic potential

9. The two conductors of a transmission line carry equal current I in opposite

directions. The force on each conductor is

(a) proportional to 7

(b) proportional to X

(c) proportional to distance between the conductors

(d) inversely proportional to I

10. A material which is slightly repelled by a magnetic field is known as

(a) ferromagnetic material

(b) diamagnetic material

(c) paramagnetic material

(d) conducting material

11. When an iron piece is placed in a magnetic field

(a) the magnetic lines of force will bend away from their usual paths in order to go

away from the piece

(b) the magnetic lines of force will bend away from their usual paths in order to
pass through the piece
(c) the magnetic field will not be affected
(d) the iron piece will break

12. Fleming's left hand rule is used to find
(a) direction of magnetic field due to current carrying conductor
(b) direction of flux in a solenoid
(c) direction of force on a current carrying conductor in a magnetic field
(d) polarity of a magnetic pole

13. The ratio of intensity of magnetisation to the magnetisation force is known as
(a) flux density
(b) susceptibility
(c) relative permeability
(d) none of the above

14. Magnetising steel is normals difficult because
(a) it corrodes easily
(6) it has high permeability
(c) it has high specific gravity
(d) it has low permeability

15. The left hand rule correlates to
(a) current, induced e.m.f. and direction of force on a conductor
(b) magnetic field, electric field and direction of force on a conductor
(c) self induction, mutual induction and direction of force on a conductor
(d) current, magnetic field and direction of force on a conductor

16. The unit of relative permeability is
(a) henry/metre
(b) henry
(c) henry/sq. m
(d) it is dimensionless

17. A conductor of length L has current I passing through it, when it is placed
parallel to a magnetic field. The force experienced by the conductor will be
(a) zero
(b) BLI

(c) B2LI

(d) BLI2

18. The force between two long parallel conductors is inversely proportional to

(a) radius of conductors

(b) current in one conductor

(c) product of current in two conductors

(d) distance between the conductors

19. Materials subjected to rapid reversal of magnetism should have

(a) large area oiB-H loop

(b) high permeability and low hysteresis loss

(c) high co-ercivity and high retentivity

(d) high co-ercivity and low density

20. Indicate which of the following material does not retain magnetism permanently.

(a) Soft iron

(b) Stainless steel

(e) Hardened steel

(d) None of the above

21. The main constituent of permalloy is

(a) cobalt

(b) chromium

(c) nickel

(d) tungsten

22. The use of permanent magnets is. not made in

(a) magnetoes

(6) energy meters

(c) transformers

(d) loud-speakers

23. Paramagnetic materials have relative permeability

(a) slightly less than unity

(b) equal to unity

(c) slightly more than unity

(d) equal to that ferromagnetic mate rials

25. Substances which have permeability less than the permeability of free space

are known as

(a) ferromagnetic

(b) paramagnetic
(c) diamagnetic
(d) bipolar

27. In the left hand rule, forefinger always represents
(a) voltage
(b) current
(c) magnetic field
(d) direction of force on the conductor

28. Which of the following is a ferromagnetic material ?
(a) Tungsten
(b) Aluminium
(c) Copper
(d) Nickel

29. Ferrites are a sub-group of
(a) non-magnetic materials
(6) ferro-magnetic materials
(c) paramagnetic materials
(d) ferri-magnetic materials

30. Gilbert is a unit of
(a) electromotive force
(b) magnetomotive force
(c) conductance
(d) permittivity

51. Unit for quantity of electricity is
(a) ampere-hour
(b) watt
(c) joule
(d) coulomb

52. The Biot-savart's law is a general modification of
(a) Kirchhoffs law
(b) Lenz's law
(c) Ampere's law
(d) Faraday's laws

53. The most effective and quickest may of making a magnet from soft iron is by
(a) placing it inside a coil carrying current
(b) induction
(c) the use of permanent magnet

(d) rubbing with another magnet

54. The commonly used material for shielding or screening magnetism is

(a) copper

(b) aluminium

(c) soft iron

(d) brass

55. If a copper disc is rotated rapidly below a freely suspended magnetic needle,

the magnetic needle shall start rotating with a velocity

(a) less than that of disc but in opposite direction

(b) equal to that of disc and in the same direction

(c) equal to that of disc and in the opposite direction

(d) less than that of disc and in the same direction

56. A permanent magnet

(a) attracts some substances and repels others

(b) attracts all paramagnetic substances and repels others

(c) attracts only ferromagnetic substances

(d) attracts ferromagnetic substances and repels all others

57. The retentivity (a property) of material is useful for the construction of

(a) permanent magnets

(b) transformers

(c) non-magnetic substances

(d) electromagnets

58. The relative permeability of materials is not constant.

(a) diamagnetic

(b) paramagnetic

(c) ferromagnetic

(d) insulating

59. The materials are a bit inferior conductors of magnetic flux than air.

(a) ferromagnetic

(b) paramagnetic

(c) diamagnetic

(d) dielectric

60. Hysteresis loop in case of magnetically hard materials is more in shape as

compared to magnetically soft materials.

(a) circular

(b) triangular

(c) rectangular

(d) none of the above

61. A rectangular magnet of magnetic moment M is cut into two piece of same

length, the magnetic moment of each piece will be

(a) M

(b) M/2

(c) 2 M

(d) M/4

62. A keeper is used to

(a) change the direction of magnetic lines

(b) amplify flux

(c) restore lost flux

(d) provide a closed path for flux

63. Magnetic moment is a

(a) pole strength

(6) universal constant

(c) scalar quantity

(d) vector quantity

64. The change of cross-sectional area of conductor in magnetic field will affect

(a) reluctance of conductor

(b) resistance of conductor

(c) (a) and (b) both in the same way

(d) none of the above

65. The uniform magnetic field is

(a) the field of a set of parallel conductors

(b) the field of a single conductor

(c) the field in which all lines of magnetic flux are parallel and equidistant

(d) none of the above

66. The magneto-motive force is

(a) the voltage across the two ends of exciting coil

(b) the flow of an electric current

(c) the sum of all currents embraced by one line of magnetic field

(d) the passage of magnetic field through an exciting coil

91. For which of the following materials the saturation value is the highest ?

(a) Ferromagnetic materials

(6) Paramagnetic materials

(c) Diamagnetic materials

(d) Ferrites

92. The magnetic materials exhibit the property of magnetisation because of

(a) orbital motion of electrons

(b) spin of electrons

(c) spin of nucleus

(d) either of these

93. For which of the following materials the net magnetic moment should be zero ?

(a) Diamagnetic materials

(b) Ferrimagnetic materials

(c) Antiferromagnetic materials

(d) Antiferrimagnetic materials

94. The attraction capacity of electromagnet will increase if the

(a) core length increases i

(b) core area increases

(c) flux density decreases

(d) flux density increases

95. Which of the following statements is correct ?

(a) The conductivity of ferrites is better than ferromagnetic materials

(b) The conductivity of ferromagnetic materials is better than ferrites

(c) The conductivity of ferrites is very high

(d) The conductivity of ferrites is same as that of ferromagnetic materials

96. Temporary magnets are used in

(a) loud-speakers

(b) generators

(c) motors

(d) all of the above

97. Main causes of noisy solenoid are

(a) strong tendency of fan out of laminations at the end caused by repulsion

among magnetic lines of force

(b) uneven bearing surface, caused by dirt or uneven wear between moving and

stationary parts

(c) both of above

(d) none of the above

99. Core of an electromagnet should have

(a) low coercivity

(6) high susceptibility

(c) both of the above

(d) none of the above

100. Magnetism of a magnet can be destroyed by

(a) heating

(b) hammering

(c) by inductive action of another magnet

(d) by all above methods

1. A semiconductor is formed by .... bonds.

A] Covalent

B] Electrovalent

C] Co-ordinate

D] None of the above

2. A semiconductor has .... temperature coefficient of resistance.

A] Positive

B] Zero

C] Negative

D] None of the above

3. The most commonly used semiconductor is ....

A] Germanium

B] Silicon

C] Carbon

D] Sulphur

6. The resistivity of a pure silicon is about ....

A] 100 O cm

B] 6000 O cm

C] 3 x 105 O m

D] 6 x 10-8 O cm

7. When a pure semiconductor is heated, its resistance ....

A] Goes up

B] Goes down

C] Remains the same

D] Can't say

8. The strength of a semiconductor crystal comes from ....

A] Forces between nuclei

B] Forces between protons

C] Electron-pair bonds

D] None of the above

9. When a pentavalent impurity is added to a pure semiconductor, it becomes ....

A] An insulator

B] An intrinsic semiconductor

C] p-type semiconductor

D] n-type semiconductor

10. Addition of pentavalent impurity to a semiconductor createsmany ....

A] Free electrons

B] Holes

C] Valence electrons

D] Bound electrons

11. A pentavalent impurity has .... Valence electrons

A] 35

B] 4

C] 6

12. An n-type semiconductor is ....

A] Positively charged

B] Negatively charged

C] Electrically neutral

D] None of the above

14. Addition of trivalent impurity to a semiconductor creates many ....

A] Holes

B] Free electrons

C] Valence electrons

D] Bound electrons

15. A hole in a semiconductor is defined as ....

A] A free electron

B] The incomplete part of an electron pair bond

C] A free proton

D] A free neutron

16. The impurity level in an extrinsic semiconductor is about ..... of pure semiconductor.

A] 10 atoms for 108 atoms

B] 1 atom for 108 atoms

C] 1 atom for 104 atoms

D] 1 atom for 100 atoms

17. As the doping to a pure semiconductor increases, the bulk resistance of the semiconductor ....

A] Remains the same

B] Increases

C] Decreases

D] None of the above

18. A hole and electron in close proximity would tend to ....

A] Repel each other

B] Attract each other

C] Have no effect on each other

D] None of the above

19. In a semiconductor, current conduction is due to ....

A] Only holes

B] Only free electrons

C] Holes and free electrons

D] None of the above

20. The random motion of holes and free electrons due to thermal agitation is called ....

A] Diffusion

B] Pressure

C] Ionisation

D] None of the above

21. A forward biased pn junction diode has a resistance of the order of

A] Ok

B] O

C] MO

D] None of the above

22. The battery connections required to forward bias a pn junction are ......

A] +ve terminal to p and –ve terminal to n

B] -ve terminal to p and +ve terminal to n

C] -ve terminal to p and –ve terminal to n

D] None of the above

23. The barrier voltage at a pn junction for germanium is about ....

A] 5 V

B] 3 V

C] Zero

D] 3 V

24. In the depletion region of a pn junction, there is a shortage of ....

A] Acceptor ions

B] Holes and electrons

C] Donor ions

D] None of the above

25. A reverse bias pn junction has ....

A] narrow depletion layer

B] Almost no current

C] Very low resistance

D] Large current flow

26. A pn junction acts as a ....

A] Controlled switch

B] Bidirectional switch

C] Unidirectional switch

D] None of the above

27. A reverse biased pn junction has resistance of the order of

A] Ok

B] O

C] MO

D] None of the above

28. The leakage current across a pn junction is due to ....

A] Minority carriers

B] Majority carriers

C] Junction capacitance

D] None of the above

29. When the temperature of an extrinsic semiconductor is increased, the pronounced effect is on......

A] Junction capacitance

B] Minority carriers

C] Majority carriers

D] None of the above

30. With forward bias to a pn junction , the width of depletion layer ....

A] Decreases

B] Increases

C] Remains the same

D] None of the above

31. The leakage current in a pn junction is of the order of

A] Aa

B] mA

C] kA

D] μA

32. In an intrinsic semiconductor, the number of free electrons ....

A] Equals the number of holes

B] Is greater than the number of holes

C] Is less than the number of holes

D] None of the above

33. At room temperature, an intrinsic semiconductor has ....

A] Many holes only

B] A few free electrons and holes

C] Many free electrons only

D] No holes or free electrons

34. At absolute temperature, an intrinsic semiconductor has ....

A] A few free electrons

B] Many holes

C] Many free electrons

D] No holes or free electrons

35. At room temperature, an intrinsic silicon crystal acts approximately as ......

A] A battery

B] A conductor

C] An insulator

D] A piece of copper wire

1. A crystal diode has ....

one pn junction

two pn junctions

three pn junctions

none of the above

ANS: 1

2. A crystal diode has forward resistance of the order of ....

kΩ

Ω
MΩ
none of the above
ANS: 2
3. If the arrow of crystal diode symbol is positive w.r.t. bar, then diode is .... biased.
forward
reverse
either forward or reverse
none of the above
ANS: 1
SEMICONDUCTOR DIODE
Questions and Answers pdf
4. The reverse current in a diode is of the order of ....
kA
mA
μA
A
ANS: 3
5. The forward voltage drop across a silicon diode is about ....
2.5 V
3 V
10 V
0.7 V
ANS: 4
6. A crystal diode is used as ....
an amplifier
a rectifier
an oscillator
a voltage regulator
ANS: 2
7. The d.c. resistance of a crystal diode is .... its a.c. resistance
the same as
more than
less than
none of the above
ANS: 3

8. An ideal crystal diode is one which behaves as a perfect .... when forward biased.
conductor
insulator
resistance material
none of the above
ANS: 1
9. The ratio of reverse resistance and forward resistance of a germanium crystal diode is about ....
1 : 1
100 : 1
1000 : 1
40,000 : 1
ANS: 4
10. The leakage current in a crystal diode is due to ....
minority carriers
majority carriers
junction capacitance
none of the above
ANS: 1
11. If the temperature of a crystal diode increases, then leakage current ....
remains the same
decreases
increases
becomes zero
ANS: 3
12. The PIV rating of a crystal diode is .... that of equivalent vacuum diode
the same as
lower than
more than
none of the above
ANS: 2
13. If the doping level of a crystal diode is increased, the breakdown voltage.............
remains the same
is increased

is decreased
none of the above
ANS: 3
14. The knee voltage of a crystal diode is approximately equal to ....
applied voltage
breakdown voltage
forward voltage
barrier potential
ANS: 4
15. When the graph between current through and voltage across a device is a straight line, the device is referred to as ....
linear
active
nonlinear
passive
ANS: 1
16. When the crystal current diode current is large, the bias is ....
forward
inverse
poor
reverse
ANS: 1
17. A crystal diode is a .... device
non-linear
bilateral
linear
none of the above
ANS: 1
18. A crystal diode utilises .... characteristic for rectification
reverse
forward
forward or reverse
none of the above
ANS: 2
19. When a crystal diode is used as a rectifier, the most important consideration is ....
forward characteristic

doping level
reverse characteristic
PIC rating
ANS: 4
20. If the doping level in a crystal diode is increased, the width of depletion layer...........
remains the same
is decreased
in increased
none of the above
ANS: 3
21. A zener diode has ....
one pn junction
two pn junctions
three pn junctions
none of the above
ANS: 1
22. A zener diode is used as ....
an amplifier
a voltage regulator
a rectifier
a multivibrator
ANS: 2
23. The doping level in a zener diode is .... that of a crystal diode
the same as
less than
more than
none of the above
ANS: 3
24. A zener diode is always .... connected.
reverse
forward
either reverse or forward
none of the above
ANS: 1
25. A zener diode utilizes .... characteristics for its operation.
forward
reverse

both forward and reverse
none of the above
ANS: 2
26. In the breakdown region, a zener didoe behaves like a .... source.
constant voltage
constant current
constant resistance
none of the above
ANS: 1
27. A zener diode is destroyed if it.............
is forward biased
is reverse biased
carrier more than rated current
none of the above
ANS: 3
28. A series resistance is connected in the zener circuit to..........
properly reverse bias the zener
protect the zener
properly forward bias the zener
none of the above
ANS: 2
29. A zener diode is .... device
a non-linear
a linear
an amplifying
none of the above
ANS: 1
30. A zener diode has .... breakdown voltage
undefined
sharp
zero
none of the above
ANS: 2
31. .... rectifier has the lowest forward resistance
solid state
vacuum tube
gas tube

none of the above

ANS: 1

32. Mains a.c. power is converrted into d.c. power for ....

lighting purposes

heaters

using in electronic equipment

none of the above

ANS: 3

33. The disadvantage of a half-wave rectifier is that the...................

components are expensive

diodes must have a higher power rating

output is difficult to filter

none of the above

ANS: 3

34. If the a.c. input to a half-wave rectifier is an r.m.s value of 400/√2 volts, then diode PIV rating is ....

400/√2 V

400 V

400 x √2 V

none of the above

ANS: 2

35. The ripple factor of a half-wave rectifier is ....

21

.21

2.5

0.48

ANS: 4

36. There is a need of transformer for ....

half-wave rectifier

centre-tap full-wave rectifier

bridge full-wave rectifier

none of the above

ANS: 2

37. The PIV rating of each diode in a bridge rectifier is .... that of the equivalent centre-tap rectifier

one-half

the same as

twice

four times
ANS: 1
38. For the same secondary voltage, the output voltage from a centretap rectifier is .... than that of bridge rectifier
twice
thrice
four time
one-half
ANS: 4
39. If the PIV rating of a diode is exceeded, ...
the diode conducts poorly
the diode is destroyed
the diode behaves like a zener diode
none of the above
ANS: 2
40. A 10 V power supply would use .... as filter capacitor.
paper capacitor
mica capacitor
electrolytic capacitor
air capacitor
ANS: 3
41. A 1,000 V power supply would use .... as a filter capacitor
paper capacitor
air capacitor
mica capacitor
electrolytic capacitor
ANS: 1
42. The .... filter circuit results in the best voltage regulation
choke input
capacitor input
resistance input
none of the above
ANS: 1
43. A half-wave rectifier has an input voltage of 240 V r.m.s. If the step-down transformer has a turns ratio of 8:1, what is the peak load voltage? Ignore diode drop.
27.5 V
86.5 V

30 V

42.5 V

ANS: 4

44. The maximum efficiency of a half-wave rectifier is ....

40.6 %

81.2 %

50 %

25 %

ANS: 1

45. The most widely used rectifier is ....

half-wave rectifier

centre-tap full-wave rectifier

bridge full-wave rectifier

none of the above

ANS:3

1. Which of the following are the applications of D.C. system ?

(a) Battery charging work

(b) Arc welding

(c) Electrolytic and electro-chemical processes

(d) Arc lamps for search lights

(e) All of the above

Ans: e

2. Which of the following methods may be used to convert A.C. system to D.C. ?

(a) Rectifiers

(b) Motor converters

(c) Motor-generator sets

(d) Rotary converters

(e) All of the above

Ans: e

3. In a single phase rotary converter the number of slip rings will be

(a) two

(b) three

(c) four

(d) six

(e) none

Ans: a

4. A synchronous converter can be started

(a) by means of a small auxiliary motor
(b) from AC. side as induction motor
(c) from D.C. side as D.C. motor
(d) any of the above methods
(e) none of the above methods
Ans: d

5. A rotary converter is a single machine with
(a) one armature and one field
(b) two armatures and one field
(c) one armature and two fields
(d) none of the above
Ans: a

6. A rotary converter combines the function of
(a) an induction motor and a D.C. generator
(b) a synchronous motor and a D.C. generator.
(c) a D.C. series motor and a D.C. generator
(d) none of the above
Ans: b

7. Which of the following is reversible in action ?
(a) Motor generator set
(b) Motor converter
(c) Rotary converter
(d) Any of the above
(e) None of the above
Ans: c

8. Which of the following metals is generally manufactured by electrolysis
process ?
(a) Load
(b) Aluminium
(c) Copper
(d) Zinc
(e) None of the above
Ans: b

9. With a motor converter it is possible to obtain D.C. voltage only upto
(a) 200-100 V
(6) 600—800 V
(c) 1000—1200 V

(d) 1700—2000 V

Ans: d

10. Normally, which of the following is used, when a large-scale conversion from

AC. to D.C. power is required ?

(a) Motor-generator set

(b) Motor converter

(c) Rotary converter

(d) Mercury arc rectifier

Ans: d

11. A rotary converter in general construction and design, is more or less like

(a) a transformer

(b) an induction motor

(c) an alternator

(d) any D.C. machine

Ans: d

12. A rotary converter operates at a

(a) low power factor

(6) high power factor

(c) zero power factor

(d) none of the above

Ans: b

13. In which of the following appUcations, direct current is absolutely essential ?

(a) Illumination

(b) Electrolysis

(c) Variable speed operation

(d) Traction

Ans: b

14. Which of the following AC. motors is usually used in large motor-generator

sets?

(a) Synchronous motor

(b) Squirrel cage induction motor

(c) Slip ring induction motor

(d) Any of the above

Ans: a

15. In a rotary converter armature currents are
(a) d.c. only
(b) a.c. only
(c) partly a.c. and partly d.c.
Ans: c
16. In which of the following equipment direct current is needed ?
(a) Telephones
(b) Relays
(c) Time switches
(d) All of the above
Ans: d
17. In a rotary converter I2R losses as compared to a D.C. generator of the same
size will be
(a) same
(b) less
(c) double
(d) three times
Ans: b
18. In a mercury arc rectifier positive ions are attracted towards
(a) anode
(b) cathode
(c) shell bottom
(d) mercury pool
Ans: b
19. Mercury, in arc rectifiers, is chosen for cathode because
(a) its ionization potential is relatively low
(b) its atomic weight is quite high
(c) its boiling point and specific heat are low
(d) it remains in liquid state at ordi¬nary temperature
(e) all of the above
Ans: e
20. The ionization potential of mercury is approximately
(a) 5.4 V
(b) 8.4 V
(c) 10.4 V
(d) 16.4 V
Ans: c

21. The potential drop in the arc, in a mercury arc rectifier, varies
(a) 0.05 V to 0.2 V per cm length of the arc
(b) 0.5 V to 1.5 V per cm length of the arc
(c) 2 V to 3.5 V per cm length of the arc
(d) none of the above
Ans: d

22. The voltage drop between the anode and cathode, of a mercury arc rectifier
comprises of the following
(a) anode drop and cathode drop
(b) anode drop and arc drop
(c) cathode drop and arc drop
(d) anode drop, cathode drop and arc drop
Ans: d

23. Glass rectifiers are usually made into units capable of D.C. output (maximum
continuous rating) of
(a) 100 A at 100 V
(b) 200 A at 200 V
(c) 300 A at 300 V
(d) 400 A at 400 V
(e) 500 A at 500 V
Ans: e

24. The voltage drop at anode, in a mercury arc rectifier is due to
(a) self restoring property of mercury
(b) high ionization potential
(c) energy spent in overcoming the electrostatic field
(d) high temperature inside the rectifier
Ans: c

25. The internal efficiency of a mercury arc rectifier depends on
(a) voltage only
(b) current only
(c) voltage and current
(d) r.m.s. value of current
(e) none of the above
Ans: a

26. If cathode and anode connections in a mercury arc rectifier are inter changed

(a) the rectifier will not operate
(b) internal losses will be reduced
(c) both ion and electron streams will move in the same direction
(d) the rectifier will operate at reduced efficiency
Ans: a

27. The cathdde voltage drop, in a mercury arc rectifier, is due to
(a) expenditure of energy in ionization
(b) surface resistance
(c) expenditure of energy in overcoming the electrostatic field
(d) expenditure of energy in liberating electrons from the mercury
Ans: d

28. To produce cathode spot in a mercury arc rectifier
(a) anode is heated
(b) tube is evacuated
(c) an auxiliary electrode is used
(d) low mercury vapour pressures are used
Ans: c

29. The advantage of mercury arc rectifier is that
(a) it is light in weight and occupies small floor space
(b) it has high efficiency
(c) it has high overload capacity
(d) it is comparatively noiseless
(e) all of the above
Ans: e

30. In a mercury pool rectifier, the voltage drop across its electrodes
(a) is directly proportional to load
(b) is inversely proportional to load
(c) varies exponentially with the load current
(d) is almost independent of load current
Ans: d

RECTIFIERS & CONVERTERS – Electrical Engineering Interview Questions
and Answers

31. In a three-phase mercury arc rectifiers each anode conducts for
(a) one-third of a cycle
(b) one-fourth of a cycle
(c) one-half a cycle
(d) two-third of a cycle

Ans: a

32. In a mercury arc rectifier characteristic blue luminosity is due to

(a) colour of mercury

(b) ionization

(c) high temperature

(d) electron streams

Ans: b

33. Which of the following mercury arc rectifier will deliver least undulating

current?

(a) Six-phase

(b) Three-phase

(c) Two-phase

(d) Single-phase

Ans: a

34. In a glass bulb mercury arc rectifier the maximum current rating is restricted

to

(a) 2000 A

(b) 1500 A

(c) 1000 A

(d) 500 A

Ans: d

35. In a mercury arc rectifier______ flow from anode to cathode

(a) ions

(b) electrons

(c) ions and electrons

(d) any of the above

Ans: a

36. When a rectifier is loaded which of the following voltage drops take place ?

(a) Voltage drop in transformer reactance

(6) Voltage drop in resistance of transformer and smoothing chokes

(c) Arc voltage drop

(d) All of the above

Ans: d

37. On which of the following factors the number of phases for which a rectifier

should be designed depend ?

(a) The voltage regulation of the rec¬tifier should be low

(b) In the output circuit there should be no harmonics

(c) The power factor of the system should be high

(d) The rectifier supply transformer should be utilized to the best advantage

(e) all of the above

Ans: e

38. A mercury arc rectifier possesses ________ regulation characteristics

(a) straight line

(b) curved line

(c) exponential

(d) none of the above

Ans: d

39. It is the________of the transformer on which the magnitude of angle of

overlap depends.

(a) resistance

(b) capacitance

(c) leakage reactance

(d) any of the above

Ans: c

41. In a grid control of mercury arc rectifiers when the grid is made positive

relative to cathode, then it the electrons on their may to anode.

(a) accelerates

(b) decelerates

(c) any of the above

(d) none of the above

Ans: a

42. In mercury arc rectifiers having grid, the arc can be struck between anode and

cathode only when the grid attains a certain potential, this potential being known

as

(a) maximum grid voltage

(b) critical grid voltage

(c) any of the above
(d) none of the above
Ans: b

43. In phase-shift control method the control is carried out by varying the of grid
voltage.
(a) magnitude
(b) polarity
(c) phase
(d) any of the above
(e) none of the above
Ans: c

16.44. In a phase-shift control method, the phase shift between anode and grid
voltages can be achieved by means of
(a) shunt motor
(6) synchronous motor
(c) induction regulator
(d) synchronous generator
Ans: c

45. The metal rectifiers are preferred to valve rectifiers due to which of the
following advantages ?
(a) They are mechanically strong
(b) They do not require any voltage for filament heating
(c) Both (a) and (b)
(d) None of the above
Ans: c

46. Which of the following statement is incorrect ?
(a) Copper oxide rectifier is a linear device
(b) Copper oxide rectifier is not a perfect rectifier
(c) Copper oxide rectifier has a low efficiency
(d) Copper oxide rectifier finds use in control circuits
(e) Copper oxide rectifier is not stable during early life
Ans: a

47. The efficiency of the copper oxide rectifier seldom exceeds
(a) 90 to 95%
(b) 85 to 90%

(c) 80 to 85%

(d) 65 to 75%

Ans: d

48. Copper oxide rectifier is usually designed not to operate above

(a) 10°C

(b) 20°C

(c) 30°C

(d) 45°C

Ans: d

49. Selenium rectifier can be operated at temperatures as high as

(a) 25°C

(b) 40°C

(c) 60°C

(d) 75°C

Ans: d

50. In selenium rectifiers efficiencies ranging from _______ to _______ percent

are attainable

(a) 25, 35

(b) 40, 50

(c) 60, 70

(d) 75, 85

Ans: d

51. Ageing of a selenium rectifier may change the output voltage by

(a) 5 to 10 per cent

(b) 15 to 20 per cent

(c) 25 to 30 per cent

(d) none of the above

Ans: a

52. The applications of selenium rectifiers are usually limited to potential of

(a) 10 V

(b) 30 V

(c) 60 V

(d) 100 V

(e) 200 V

Ans: d

53. Which of the following rectifiers have been used extensively in supplying
direct current for electroplating ?
(a) Copper oxide rectifiers
(b) Selenium rectifiers
(c) Mercury arc rectifiers
(d) Mechanical rectifiers
(e) None of the above
Ans: b
54. A commutating rectifier consists of commutator driven by
(a) an induction motor
(b) a synchronous motor
(c) a D.C. series motor
(d) a D.C. shunt motor
Ans: b
55. Which of the following rectifiers are primarily used for charging of low voltage
batteries from AC. supply ?
(a) Mechanical rectifiers
(b) Copper oxide rectifiers
(c) Selenium rectifiers
(d) Electrolytic rectifiers
(e) Mercury arc rectifiers
Ans: d
56. The efficiency of an electrolytic rectifier is nearly
(a) 80%
(b) 70%
(c) 60%
(d) 40%
Ans: c
57. Which of the following is the loss within the mercury arc rectifier chamber ?
(a) Voltage drop in arc
(6) Voltage drop at the anode
(c) Voltage drop at the cathode
(d) All of the above
Ans: d
58. The metal rectifiers, as compared to mercury arc rectifiers

(a) operate on low temperatures
(b) can operate on high voltages
(c) can operate on heavy loads
(d) give poor regulation
(e) none of the above
Ans: a

59. In a mercury arc rectifier, the anode is usually made of
(a) copper
(b) aluminium
(c) silver
(d) graphite
(e) tungsten
Ans: d

1. Which of the following does not change in a transformer ?
(a) Current
(b) Voltage
(c) Frequency
(d) All of the above

2. In a transformer the energy is conveyed from primary to secondary
(a) through cooling coil
(b) through air
(c) by the flux
(d) none of the above

3. A transformer core is laminated to
(a) reduce hysteresis loss
(b) reduce eddy current losses
(c) reduce copper losses
(d) reduce all above losses

4. The degree of mechanical vibrations produced by the laminations of a transformer depends on
(a) tightness of clamping
(b) gauge of laminations
(c) size of laminations
(d) all of the above

5. The no-load current drawn by transformer is usually what per cent of the full load current ?
(a) 0.2 to 0.5 per cent
(b) 2 to 5 per cent

(c) 12 to 15 per cent
(d) 20 to 30 per cent

6. The path of a magnetic flux in a transformer should have
(a) high resistance
(b) high reluctance
(c) low resistance
(d) low reluctance

7. No-load on a transformer is carried out to determine
(a) copper loss
(b) magnetising current
(c) magnetising current and loss
(d) efficiency of the transformer

8. The dielectric strength of transformer oil is expected to be
(a) lkV
(b) 33 kV
(c) 100 kV
(d) 330 kV

9. Sumpner's test is conducted on trans-formers to determine
(a) temperature
(b) stray losses
(c) all-day efficiency
(d) none of the above

10. The permissible flux density in case of cold rolled grain oriented steel is around
(a) 1.7 Wb/m2
(b) 2.7 Wb/m2
(c) 3.7 Wb/m2
(d) 4.7 Wb/m2

11. The efficiency of a transformer will be maximum when
(a) copper losses = hysteresis losses
(b) hysteresis losses = eddy current losses
(c) eddy current losses = copper losses
(d) copper losses = iron losses

12. No-load current in a transformer
(a) lags behind the voltage by about 75°
(b) leads the voltage by about 75°
(c) lags behind the voltage by about 15°
(d) leads the voltage by about 15°

13. The purpose of providing an iron core in a transformer is to

(a) provide support to windings

(b) reduce hysteresis loss

(c) decrease the reluctance of the magnetic path

(d) reduce eddy current losses

14. Which of the following is not a part of transformer installation ?

(a) Conservator

(b) Breather

(c) Buchholz relay

(d) Exciter

15. While conducting short-circuit test on a transformer the following side is short circuited

(a) High voltage side

(b) Low voltage side

(c) Primary side

(d) Secondary side

16. In the transformer following winding has got more cross-sectional area

(a) Low voltage winding

(b) High voltage winding

(c) Primary winding

(d) Secondary winding

17. A transformer transforms

(a) voltage

(b) current

(c) power

(d) frequency

18. A transformer cannot raise or lower the voltage of a D.C. supply because

(a) there is no need to change the D.C. voltage

(b) a D.C. circuit has more losses

(c) Faraday's laws of electromagnetic induction are not valid since the rate of change of flux is zero

(d) none of the above

19. Primary winding of a transformer

(a) is always a low voltage winding

(b) is always a high voltage winding

(c) could either be a low voltage or high voltage winding

(d) none of the above

20. Which winding in a transformer has more number of turns ?

(a) Low voltage winding

(b) High voltage winding

(c) Primary winding

(d) Secondary winding

21. Efficiency of a power transformer is of the order of

(a) 100 per cent

(b) 98 per cent

(c) 50 per cent

(d) 25 per cent

22. In a given transformer for given applied voltage, losses which remain constant irrespective of load changes are

(a) friction and windage losses

(b) copper losses

(c) hysteresis and eddy current losses

(d) none of the above

23. A common method of cooling a power transformer is

(a) natural air cooling

(b) air blast cooling

(c) oil cooling

(d) any of the above

24. The no load current in a transformer lags behind the applied voltage by an angle of about

(a) 180°

(b) 120″

(c) 90°

(d) 75°

25. In a transformer routine efficiency depends upon

(a) supply frequency

(b) load current

(c) power factor of load

(d) both (b) and (c)

26. In the transformer the function of a conservator is to

(a) provide fresh air for cooling the transformer

(b) supply cooling oil to transformer in time of need

(c) protect the transformer from damage when oil expends due to heating

(d) none of the above
27. Natural oil cooling is used for transformers up to a rating of
(a) 3000 kVA
(b) 1000 kVA
(c) 500 kVA
(d) 250 kVA
28. Power transformers are designed to have maximum efficiency at
(a) nearly full load
(b) 70% full load
(c) 50% full load
(d) no load
29. The maximum efficiency of a distribution transformer is
(a) at no load
(b) at 50% full load
(c) at 80% full load
(d) at full load
30. Transformer breaths in when
(a) load on it increases
(b) load on it decreases
(c) load remains constant
(d) none of the above
31. No-load current of a transformer has
(a) has high magnitude and low power factor
(b) has high magnitude and high power factor
(c) has small magnitude and high power factor
(d) has small magnitude and low power factor
32. Spacers are provided between adjacent coils
(a) to provide free passage to the cooling oil
(b) to insulate the coils from each other
(c) both (a) and (b)
(d) none of the above
33. Greater the secondary leakage flux
(a) less will be the secondary induced e.m.f.
(b) less will be the primary induced e.m.f.
(c) less will be the primary terminal voltage
(d) none of the above
34. The purpose of providing iron core in a step-up transformer is
(a) to provide coupling between primary and secondary

(b) to increase the magnitude of mutual flux

(c) to decrease the magnitude of mag-netizing current

(d) to provide all above features

35. The power transformer is a constant

(a) voltage device

(b) current device

(c) power device

(d) main flux device

36. Two transformers operating in parallel will share the load depending upon their

(a) leakage reactance

(b) per unit impedance

(c) efficiencies

(d) ratings

37. If R2 is the resistance of secondary winding of the transformer and K is the transformation ratio then the equivalent secondary resistance referred to primary will be

(a) R2/VK

(b) R2IK2

(c) R22!K2

(d) R22/K

38. What will happen if the transformers working in parallel are not connected with regard to polarity ?

(a) The power factor of the two trans-formers will be different from the power factor of common load

(b) Incorrect polarity will result in dead short circuit

(c) The transformers will not share load in proportion to their kVA ratings

(d) none of the above

39. If the percentage impedances of the two transformers working in parallel are different, then

(a) transformers will be overheated

(b) power factors of both the transformers will be same

(c) parallel operation will be not possible

(d) parallel operation will still be possible, but the power factors at which the two transformers operate will be different from the power factor of the common load

40. In a transformer the tappings are generally provided on

(a) primary side

(b) secondary side

(c) low voltage side

(d) high voltage side

41. The use of higher flux density in the transformer design

(a) reduces weight per kVA

(6) reduces iron losses

(c) reduces copper losses

(d) increases part load efficiency

42. The chemical used in breather for transformer should have the quality of

(a) ionizing air

(b) absorbing moisture

(c) cleansing the transformer oil

(d) cooling the transformer oil.

43. The chemical used in breather is

(a) asbestos fiber

(b) silica sand

(c) sodium chloride

(d) silica gel

45. The transformer ratings are usually expressed in terms of

(a) volts

(b) amperes

(c) kW

(d) kVA

46. The noise resulting from vibrations of laminations set by magnetic forces, is termed as

(a) magnetostrication

(b) boo

(c) hum

(d) zoom

47. Hysteresis loss in a transformer varies as CBmax = maximum flux density)

(a) Bmax

(b) Bmax1-6

(C) Bmax1-83

(d) B max

48. Material used for construction of transformer core is usually

(a) wood
(b) copper
(c) aluminium
(d) silicon steel
49. The thickness of laminations used in a transformer is usually
(a) 0.4 mm to 0.5 mm
(b) 4 mm to 5 mm
(c) 14 mm to 15 mm
(d) 25 mm to 40 mm
50. The function of conservator in a transformer is
(a) to project against'internal fault
(b) to reduce copper as well as core losses
(c) to cool the transformer oil
(d) to take care of the expansion and contraction of transformer oil due to variation of temperature of sur-roundings
51. The highest voltage for transmitting electrical power in India is
(a) 33 kV.
(6) 66 kV
(c) 132 kV
(d) 400 kV
52. In a transformer the resistance between its primary and secondary is
(a) zero
(b) 1 ohm
(c) 1000 ohms
(d) infinite
53. A transformer oil must be free from
(a) sludge
(b) odour
(c) gases
(d) moisture
54. A Buchholz relay can be installed on
(a) auto-transformers
(b) air-cooled transformers
(c) welding transformers
(d) oil cooled transformers
55. Gas is usually not liberated due to dissociation of transformer oil unless the oil temperature exceeds
(a) 50°C

(b) 80°C

(c) 100°C

(d) 150°C

56. The main reason for generation of harmonics in a transformer could be

(a) fluctuating load

(b) poor insulation

(c) mechanical vibrations

(d) saturation of core

57. Distribution transformers are generally designed for maximum efficiency around

(a) 90% load

(b) zero load

(c) 25% load

(d) 50% load

58. Which of the following property is not necessarily desirable in the material for transformer core ?

(a) Mechanical strength

(6) Low hysteresis loss

(c) High thermal conductivity

(d) High permeability

59. Star/star transformers work satisfactorily when

(a) load is unbalanced only

(b) load is balanced only

(c) on balanced as well as unbalanced loads

(d) none of the above

60. Delta/star transformer works satisfactorily when

(a) load is balanced only

(b) load is unbalanced only

(c) on balanced as well as unbalanced loads

(d) none of the above

61. Buchholz's relay gives warning and protection against

(a) electrical fault inside the transformer itself

(b) electrical fault outside the transformer in outgoing feeder

(c) for both outside and inside faults

(d) none of the above

62. The magnetising current of a transformer is usually small because it has

(a) small air gap
(b) large leakage flux
(c) laminated silicon steel core
(d) fewer rotating parts

63. Which of the following does not change in an ordinary transformer ?
(a) Frequency
(b) Voltage
(c) Current
(d) Any of the above

64. Which of the following properties is not necessarily desirable for the material for transformer core ?
(a) Low hysteresis loss
(b) High permeability
(c) High thermal conductivity
(d) Adequate mechanical strength

65. The leakage flux in a transformer depends upon
(a) load current
(b) load current and voltage
(c) load current, voltage and frequency
(d) load current, voltage, frequency and power factor

66. The path of the magnetic flux in transformer should have
(a) high reluctance
(b) low reactance
(c) high resistance
(d) low resistance

67. Noise level test in a transformer is a
(a) special test
(b) routine test
(c) type test
(d) none of the above

68. Which of the following is not a routine test on transformers ?
(a) Core insulation voltage test
(b) Impedance test
(c) Radio interference test
(d) Polarity test

69. A transformer can have zero voltage regulation at
(a) leading power factor
(b) lagging power factor

(c) unity power factor

(d) zero power factor

70. Helical coils can be used on

(a) low voltage side of high kVA transformers

(b) high frequency transformers

(c) high voltage side of small capacity transformers

(d) high voltage side of high kVA rating transformers

1. Processor, main memory (RAM), hard disk, CD/DVD drive, CMOS, BIOS chip, etc. are housed inside ______.

(a) input unit

(b) Central Processing Unit (CPU)

(c) output unit

(d) all of them

2. _______ contains slots for fixing/ connecting processor, main memory (RAM), hard disk, CD/DVD drive, CMOS, BIOS chip, etc.

(a) Mother board

(b) bread board

(c) key board

(d) dash board

3. A stylus used to provide input through CRT monitor is called ________.

(a) scanner

(b) digital tablet

(c) light pen

(d) printer

4. VDU is expanded as _______.

(a) Visual Display Unit

(b) Virtual Display Unit (c) Visual Deception Unit

(d) Visual Display University

5. In computer monitors, CRT stands for ______.

(a) Cadmium Ray Tube

(b) Cathode Ray Tube

(c) Cathode Ray Twist

(d) Cathode Rim

6. Cathode Ray Tube (CRT) monitor has _______ level of power consumption amongst monitors.

(a) highest

(b) lowest

(c) zero

(d) least

7. LCD is expanded as ______.

(a) Linear Crystal Display

(b) Liquid Crystal Dialog

(c) Liquid Crystal Display

(d) Liquid Canister Display

8. LED is expanded as ________.

(a) Linear Emitting Diode

(b) Light Emitting Diode

(c) Liquid Emitting Diode

(d) Light Emitting Display

9. The display of LCD monitor is _______ than that of LED monitor.

(a) lighter

(b) heavier

(c) brighter

(d) duller

10. Height to width ratio of a monitor screen is called _______.

(a) aspect ratio

(b) length ratio

(c) width ratio

(d) diagonal ratio

11. Generally, CRT monitors had aspect ratio of _______.

(a) 16:9

(b) 4:3

(c) 16:10

(d) 1:1

12. The type of printer which hits the paper to produce print is called ______.

(a) monitor

(b) scanner

(c) non-impact type printer

(d) impact type printer

13. The type of printer which does not hit the paper to produce print is called _______.

(a) monitor

(b) scanner

(c) non-impact type printer

(d) impact type printer

14. Dot matrix printer belongs to ________ category.
(a) monitor
(b) scanner
(c) non-impact type printer
(d) impact type printer

15. LASER printer, ink jet printer, thermal printer and plotter belong to _____ category.
(a) monitor
(b) scanner
(c) non-impact type printer
(d) impact type printer

16. Thermal printer uses _______ coated paper, which turns black when heat is applied.
(a) chromium
(b) BisPhenol
(c) nickel
(d) toner powder

17. The unit which splits power supply to various voltages required for their units of a computer is called ______ .
(a) transformer
(b) Switch Mode Power Supply (SMPS)
(c) transistor
(d) transducer

18. Full form for SMPS in computer is ______.
(a) Sync Mode Power Supply
(b) Switch Mode Power Supply
(c) Stake Mode Power Supply
(d) Switch Mode Power Socket

19. In a desktop computer, ______ produces radio frequency interference.
(a) SMPS
(b) Micro-Processor
(c) RAM
(d) Mouse

20. The opening provided in the front panel or rear panel of a CPU for connecting peripherals is called ______.
(a) socket
(b) pin
(c) port

(d) part

21. External dialup MODEM can be connected to a computer using ______ port.

(a) <u>RS232/ serial</u>

(b) PS/2

(c) VGA

(d) LPT

22. Old style (SIMPLEX) printer (like dot matrix printer) may be connected to a computer using _____ port.

(a) RS232/ serial

(b) PS/2

(c) VGA

(d) <u>LPT</u>

23. Modern (DUPLEX) printer (like LASER jet, inkjet printers) may be connected to a computer using ______ port.

(a) RS232/

(b) <u>USB</u>

(c) PS/2

(d) VGA

24. Broadband connection may be connected through _____ port.

(a) <u>RJ45/ Ethernet</u>

(b) USB

(c) PS/2

(d) VGA

25. Printer, fax machine, scanner, web camera, external DVD writer, external hard disk, etc. can be connected to computer using ______ port.

(a) RJ45

(b) <u>USB</u>

(c) PS/2

(d) VGA

26. Joystick can be connected to computer using ______ port.

(a) 3.5mm jack

(b) RJ11

(c) RJ45

(d) <u>Game</u>

27. PS/2 stands for ______.

(a) Registered Jack 11

(b) Registered Jack 45

(c) Personal System 2
(d) Recommended Standard 232
28. RJ11 stands for ______.
(a) Registered Jack 11
(b) Registered Jack 45
(c) Personal System 2
(d) Recommended Standard 232
29. RJ45 stands for ______ .
(a) Registered Jack 11
(b) Registered Jack 45
(c) Personal System 2
(d) Recommended Standard
30. RS232 stands for ______.
(a) Registered Jack 11
(b) Registered Jack 45
(c) Personal System 2
(d) Recommended Standard 232
31. RJ45 port is otherwise called _______.
(a) Ethernet
(b) LPT
(c) USB
(d) VGA
32. IEEE 1392 port is otherwise called _______
(a) Ethernet
(b) LPT
(c) USB
(d) Firewire
33. LPT stands for ______.
(a) Registered Jack 11
(b) Registered Jack 45
(c) Line Printer Terminal
(d) Recommended Standard 232
34. USB stands for _______.
(a) Registered Jack 11
(b) Registered Jack 45
(c) Line Printer Terminal
(d) Universal Serial Bus
35. High definition graphics output may be taken from port of a PC.

(a) 3.5mm jack

(b) HDMI

(c) RJ45

(d) LPT

36. HDMI stands for

(a) Registered Jack

(b) High Definition Multimedia Interface

(c) Line Printer Terminal

(d) Universal Serial Bus

37. The device primarily used to provide hardcopy is the

a) CRT

b) Computer Console

c) Printer

d) Card Reader

38. Dot-matrix, Deskjet, Inkjet and Laser are all types of which computer peripherals?

a) Printers

b) Software

c) Monitors

d) Keyboards

39. Laser printer belong to

a) line printer

b) page printer

c) band printer

d) dot matrix printer

40. A joystick is primarily used for

a) control sound on the screen

b) Computer gaming

c) enter text

d) draw pictures

41. USB refers to

a) a storage

b) a processor

c) a port type

d) a serial bus standard

42. The ___ may also be called the screen or monitor.

a) printer

b) scanner

c) hard disk

d) <u>display</u>

43. Speed of the printer is limited by the speed of

a) paper movement

b) <u>cartridge used</u>

c) length of paper

d) all of these

44. The OCR recognizes the ___ of the characters with the help of light source.

a) size

b) <u>shape</u>

c) colour

d) used ink

45. Laser printer belong to

a) Line printer

b) <u>page printer</u>

c) band printer

d) dot matrix printer

46. A device used for video games, flight simulators, training simulators and for controlling industrial robots.

a) Mouse

b) Light pen

c) <u>Joystick</u>

d) keyboard

47. The unattached interactive information systems such as automatic teller machine or ATM is called as _____

a) <u>Kiosks</u>

b) Sioks

c) Cianto

d) Kiaks

48. _____ help prevent power surges.

a) <u>Surge suppressor</u>

b) Spike protector

c) UPS system

d) High-grade multi-meter

49. If the memory slots have 30 pins then the chip is a?

a) DIMM

b) <u>SIMM</u>

c) SDRAM

d) All of these

50. Laser jet printer speeds are measured in pages per minute (ppm) what do we use to measure dot-matrix printers?

a) lines per inch

b) lines per sheet

c) characters per inch

d) characters per second

51. For a Macintosh to print successfully, the System Folder must contain:

a) File sharing software

b) A printer enabler

c) The apple Garamond font set

d) A printer driver

52. Which component must be vacuumed or replaced during preventative maintenance on a laserprinter?

a) Scanning mirror

b) Toner cartridge

c) Ozone filter

d) All of these

53. Which device uses a DMA channel?

a) Modem

b) Network Card

c) Sound Card

d) All of these

54.A modem could be attached to which port?

a) Parallel port

b) ASYNC port

c) Keyboard connector

d) Video port

55. What device prevents power interruptions, resulting in corrupted data?

a) Battery back-up unit

b) Surge protector

c) Multiple SIMMs strips

d) Data guard system

56. SCSI must be terminated with?

a) Dip switch

b) Resister

c) BNC

d) All of these

57. What?s the best way to prevent damaging your PC with static electricity?

a) place your PC on a rubber mat

b) wear leather soled shoes

c) periodically touch a safe ground point on the PC to discharge yourself

d) wear an ESD wrist strap

58. Which would you do first when troubleshooting a faulty monitor?

a) Check its connections to the computer and power source

b) Power down the monitor, then turn it on again to see if that corrects the problem

c) Use a meter to check the CRT and internal circuitry for continuity

d) None of these

59. What do you need to check serial and parallel port?

a) Port adapter

b) Logic probe

c) Loopback plug

d) All of these

60. You have a PC with no video* Which of the following is LEAST likely to be causing the problem?

a) defective RAM (bank zero)

b) defective microprocessor

c) crashed hard drive

d) loose video card

61. You get a CMOS checksum error during bootup. What is most likely the cause?

a) Power supply is bad

b) BIOS needs updating

c) CMOS battery is nearing end of life

d) None of these

62. Which should you use for cleaning Mylar-protected LCD screens?

a) Ammonia window cleaner

b) Non-abrasive cleanser

c) Anti-static wipes

d) Alcohol-impregnated wipes

63. What could cause a fixed disk error?

a) No-CD installed
b) Bad Ram
c) Slow processor
d) Incorrect CMOS settings

64. What is the most significant difference between the USB and IEEE 1394 standards?

a) IEEE 1394 is faster
b) USB does not support
c) USB is plug and play
d) IEEE 1394 is not swappable

65. When connecting two internal SCSI hard disks to a computer, where do you connect the second hard drive?

a) Any open SCSI port on the computer
b) A serial port on the first host adapter
c) An open parallel port on the computer
d) An open SCSI port on the first hard drive

66. When connecting a ribbon cable to a connector, how do you know which direction to plug it in?

a) The red line in the cable goes to the highest pin number
b) The colored line in the cable goes to pin #1
c) It does not matter
d) None of these

67. What is the first step in diagnosing a completely dead computer at the client site that was working the day before.

a) Test the power supply
b) replace the CMOS battery
c) check the AC outlet
d) reseat the hard drive controller cable

68. What specification covers PC hard cards?

a) SCSI
b) ISA
c) PCMCIA
d) MFM

69. Which common bus specification provides the fastest data transfer rate?

a) VL bus
b) ISA
c) PCI

d) All of these

70. Modems use transmission.

a) Synchronous

b) Asynchronous

c) timed interval

d) ata

71. A 6xx indicates a problem with the:

a) floppy drive

b) hard drive

c) keyboard

d) CD ROM

72. During preventative maintenance on a dot matrix printer, do NOT lubricate:

a) Platen assembly

b) Print head pulley

c) Print head pins

d) Paper advance gear bushings

73. You see the message “invalid media device” after installing a new hard drive. What do you do next?

a) Format

b) Fdisk

c) Partition

d) Add the OS

74. A workstation has just been installed on an Ethernet LAN, but cannot communicate with the network. What should you check first?

a) reinstall the network protocols

b) reinstall the network interface card driver

c) verify the ip configuration on the workstation

d) verify the link status on the computers network card

75. One of the major components of a PC is the Central Processing Unit (CPU) Which can be best described as:

a) The device that sends the monitor signals telling it what to display

b) The area that regulates all of the system power usage

c) The area where ail the of the Basic input/output routines are stored

d) The area where all of the processing takes place

76. Which monitor would provide the highest level of performance?

a) VGA

b) XGA

c) CGA
d) SVGA

77. Which of the following items would require you to comply with EPA disposal guidelines?
a) Keyboard
b) System board
c) Power supply
d) Battery

78. A hard disk is divided into tracks which are further subdivided into:
a) clusters
b) sectors
c) vectors
d) heads

79. What is the paper feeding technology most commonly associated with dot-matrix printers?
a) sheet feed
b) tractor feed
c) friction feed
d) manual feed

80. Which step should you perform first before discharging a CRT?
a) Remove the CRT from its housing
b) Disconnect the CRT from the computer
c) Remove the video assembly
d) Turn power off before removing power source

81. A capacitor is measured in which of the following units?
a) Volts
b) Ohms
c) Farads
d) Resistance

82. What would you ask to determine if the display is working?
a) Is there a video cursor or action on the screen?
b) Did the computer beep or chime?
c) Is there high voltage static on the screen
d) All of these

83. Your CD-ROM audio cable connects to the:
a) speaker
b) sound card (or motherboard if sound is integrated with it)
c) power supply

d) hard drive

84. Type one PC cards:

a) are used only in desktops

b) are no longer being produced

c) are the thinnest of the PC cards

d) don?t exist

85. In laser technology, what happens during the transfer stage? a) Residual toner is transferred to the waste receptacle

b) The laser transfers the image from the drum to the paper

c) The image is transferred from the drum to the paper

d) A negative charge is transferred to the surface to the drum

86. Suppose that the power lamp is on, but the printer will not print. What can you do to correct the problem?

a) Make sure the printer is on line

b) Replace the AC line fuse

c) Turn the printer on and off

d) Replace the ribbon

87. A dialog box with a bomb appears on a Macintosh screen. What type of problem has occurred?

a) A RAM problem

b) A software problem

c) A ROM problem

d) An ADB problem

88. What can you use to ensure power is not interrupted, resulting in corrupted data?

a) UPS

b) Propergrounding

c) Surge protector

d) Sag protector

89. A 25-pin female connector on the back of your computer will typically be:

a) Serial port 1

b) A parallel port

c) Docking

d) COM2 port

90. What is the recommended way to fix the registry description for the printer driver

a) Delete the spool file

b) Run regedit.exe and remove any reference to the printers

c) Run sysedit.exe and remove any reference to the printers

d) Remove the printer driver and re-install it

91. An important first step in troubleshooting which component in a laser printer is causing a jam is to:

a) note where in the paper path the paper stops

b) check all voltages

c) look up error codes

d) turn the printer off, then on again

92. What is the size of the reserved memory area?

a) 64 kb

b) 384 kb

c) 640 kb

d) 1024 kb

93. Dust in a computer actually increase the size of the magnetic fields inside it. This is not good, so you must occasionaly dust, I trust. What?s the best way to do this?

a) reservevaccum

b) any small vaccum device

c) blow real hard on the system board

d) use compressed air can

94. A parity error usually indicates a problem with:

a) memory

b) hard drive

c) hard drive controller

d) I/O controller

95. The monitor power LED is „on? but the monitor screen is completely dark. The least likely cause of the problem is:

a) Defect in the computers video circuitry

b) Disconnected video cable

c) Defective monitor

d) System RAM problem

96. How is ink transferred to paper in common ink jet printers?

a) Boiling ink

b) Crystal

c) Motorized pump

d) Ink is sprayed on the paper and managed by a nozzle

97. In Inkjet printers, what is the most common problem with the paper tray?

a) inconsistent printing

b) <u>malfunctioning pick-up rollers</u>

c) misalignment of the sheet feeder

d) paper jamming on the ink cartridge

98. A customer calls and says her computer won?t boot, she can hear noises and can see lights on the box, but nothing comes up on the screen, what should you take to the site to fix the problem?

a) hard drive

b) <u>video card</u>

c) power cable

d) power supply

99. What action will correct patchy, faint, uneven or intermittent print on a dot matrix printer?

a) <u>Replacing the ribbon</u>

b) Replacing the timing belt

c) Adjusting the paper feed tension

d) Adjusting the tractor feed ransion

100. Every video card must have?

a) CMOS

b) <u>RAM</u>

c) CPU

d) All of these

101. Which best describes a fragmented hard drive:

a) The platters are bad

b) Data files are corrupted

c) Clusters of data are damaged

d) <u>Files are not stored in consecutive clusters</u>

102. A laser printer generates a totally black page, what is the cause?

a) malfunctioning imaging laser

b) low level in the toner cartridge

c) no power to transfer corona

d) <u>no power to the primary corona</u>

103. You must service the laser printer in your office. Which part of the printer should you avoid touching because it is hot?

a) <u>Fuser</u>

b) Printer head

c) primary corona
d) High voltage power supply

104. During the normal PC boot process, which of the following is active first?
a) RAM BIOS
b) CMOS
c) ROM BIOS
d) Hard disk information

105. Which device should not be plugged into a standard ups?
a) monitor
b) laser printer
c) ink-jet printer
d) an external modem

106. What allows you to print on both sides of the printer?
a) fuser
b) duplexer
c) toner cartridge
d) paper-swapping unit

107. Which is NOT typically a field Replaceable Unit?
a) System ROM
b) Power supply
c) System chasis
d) Video controller

108. Which is the easiest component to environmentally recycle?
a) Motherboards
b) CMOS batteries
c) Toner cartridges
d) Cathode ray tubes

109. What problem can occur if a printer cable is to close to a power cable?
a) ESD Electrostatic Discharge
b) EMI Electromagnetic Interference
c) parity error
d) no affect

110. How can you totally protect a PC from damage during an electrical storm?
a) Disconnect the AC power cable
b) Disconnect all external cables and power cords

c) Use a surge protector

d) Turn off the AC power

111. All operating systems get their total memory initialized from? a) CPU

b) <u>BIOS</u>

c) ROM

d) RAM

112. During the fusing process, toner is:

a) dry pressed into the paper

b) electrically bonded to the paper

c) melted into the paper

d) <u>high pressure sprayed onto the paper</u>

113. After you service a laser printer, you notice dirty print. Which of the following would correct the problem?

a) Clean the developer tank

b) Reset the printer

c) <u>Run several blank pages</u>

d) Clean the laser diode

114. During the boot process, a system first counts memory from where?

a) Expansion memory board

b) Video adapter

c) <u>System board</u>

d) Cache

115. You have a system that periodically locks up. You have ruled out software, and now suspect that it is hardware. What should you do first that could help you narrow it down to the component at fault?

a) rotate the RAM

b) replace the RAM

c) replace the level 2 cache SIMM

d) <u>disable the CPU cache in CMOS</u>

116. What is the best way to protect your hard drive data?

a) <u>regular backups</u>

b) periodically defrag it

c) runchkdsk at least once a week

d) run a regular diagnostic

117. Missing slot covers on a computer can cause?

a) <u>over heat</u>

b) power surges

c) EMI

d) incomplete path for ESD

118. In laser printer technology, what happens during the conditioning stage?

a) The corona wire places a uniform positive charge on the paper

b) A uniform negative charge is placed on the photosensitive drum

c) A uniform negative charge is placed on the toner

d) All of these

119. What product is used to clean keys on a keyboard?

a) TMC solvent

b) Silicon spray

c) Denatured alcohol

d) All-purpose cleaner

120. Which peripheral port provide the FASTEST throughout to laser printers?

a) RS-232

b) SCSI

c) Parallel

d) Serial

121. Your customer tells you the print quality of their dot matrix printer is light then dark. Which of the following could cause the problem.

a) Paper slippage

b) Improper ribbon advancement

c) Paper thickness

d) Head position

122. The 34-pin connection on an I/O card I for?

a) Floppy drive

b) SCSI drive

c) IDE drive

d) Zip drive

123. The terms "red book", "yellow book" and "orange book" refer to:

a) SCSI

b) IDE

c) Floppy drive technology

d) CD-ROM standards

124. What beep codes could indicate a system board or power supply failure?

a) steady short beep

b) no beep
c) one long continuous beep tone
d) All of these

125. Which part of the laser printer should NOT be exposed to sunlight?
a) Transfer corona assembly
b) PC drum
c) Primary corona wire
d) Toner cartridge

126. In inkjet technology the droplets on ink are deflected by?
a) multi directional nozzles
b) electronically charges plates
c) high pressure plates
d) electro static absorbtion

127. Which provide the fastest access to large video files?
a) Optical drives
b) IDE hard drives
c) SCSI hard drives
d) EIDE hard drives

128. A 25-pin female connector on the back of your computer will typically be:
a) Serial port 1
b) A parallel port
c) Docking
d) COM2 port

129. On the PC side, the printer port is a:
a) 25 pin female serial connector
b) 15 pin female parallel connector
c) 25 pin male serial connector
d) 25 pin female parallel connector

130. You are installing an application in Windows 95, and the computer crashes, what do you do?
a) Press alt + Ctrl + delete, twice
b) press alt + Ctrl + delete, and end task
c) press the reset button on the computer
d) turn off computer and boot from a floppy disk

131. RS-232 is a standard that applies to:
a) serial ports
b) parallel ports

c) game ports

d) networks

132. You just installed a new IDE hard drive, but your system BIOS will not recognize the new drive, what should you check first.

a) cable sequence

b) <u>jumpers on the hard drive</u>

c) drivers that need to be loaded

d) hard drive manufacturer web site information

133. All the physical components of a computer are collectively called .

(a) software

(b) <u>hardware</u>

(c) malware

(d) junkware

134. Hardware ______ be touched.

(a) cannot

(b) <u>can</u>

(c) may

(d) would

135. Hardware ______ electric power for working.

(a) <u>consumes</u>

(b) does not consume

(c) generates (d) creates

136. Hardware ______ space.

(a) does not occupy

(b) <u>occupies</u>

(c) does not require

(d) does not need

Q.1. Which of the following is the biggest unit of memory?

A] <u>Gigabytes.</u>

B] bytes.

C] Megabytes.

D] Kilobytes.

Q.2. The primary purpose of software is to turn data into.

A] Website.

B] <u>Infromation.</u>

C] Programs.

D] Objects.

Q.3. GUI Stands for

A] Graphical User Interface.

B] Greater User Interface.

C] Graphical Union Interface.

D] Graphical User Intereat.

Q.4. Key board keys that have arrows on them are called -

A] Function Keys.

B] Navigation Keys.

C] Typewriter Keys.

D] Special purpose keys.

Q.5. ASSCII, EBCDIC and Unicode are examples of Application Software's

A] True.

B] False.

Q.6. The easiest way to access any part of the screen in the windows operating system is using the.

A] Key Board.

B] Rat.

C] Mouse.

D]] Joystick.

Q.7. A software is also called as a

A] Procedure.

B] Data.

C] Programs.

D] Information.

Q.8. Back programs make copies of the files to be used in case the original files are damaged or lost.

A] True.

B] False.

Q.9. Microprocessor is often called as CPU

A] True.

B] False.

Q.10. .... Utility identifies unnecessary files on the hard disk and erases them based on users command.

A] Backup.

B] File Compression.

C] Uninstall Programs.

D]] Disk Clean up.

Q.11. This type of software is designs to help you be more productive tasks, and is widely used in nearly every disc live and occupation.

A] Communication Software.

B] Utility Software.

C] Basic Application Software.

D] System Software.

Q.12. Minicomputers are also known as.

A] Mid Range Computers.

B] Personal Digital Computers.

C] Mainframe Computers.

D] Laptop Computers.

Q.13. Which of the following device is used to play fast games on a computers.

A] Touch Surface.

B] Touch Screen.2

C] Track Ball.

D] Joystick.

Q.14. Which of the following would not be considered as portable computer.

A] Desktop Computer.

B] Note book computer.

C] Personal Digital Assistant.

D] None of these.

Q.15. Headphone is a typical output device.

A] True.

B] False.

Q.16. Uninstall programs help us to remove unwanted programs installed in the computer.

A] True.

B] False.

Q.17. The capacity of a storage device is usually measured in terms of bytes.

A] True.

B] False.

Q.18. Capacity of the storage device is usually measured in terms of meter.

A] True.

B] False.

Q.19............. is a pointing device.

A] Mouse.

B] Printer.

C] Scanner.

D] Keyboard.

Q.20. The keyboards keys that are labelled F1, F2 and so on are called ....

A] Function Keys.

B] Numeric Keys.

C] Typewriter Keys.

D] Special purpose keys.

Q.21. The keyboard keys like Caps lock that turn on features on or off are called.

A] Function Keys.

B] Combination Keys.

C] Toggle Keys.

D] Special Purpose Keys.

Q.22. Word processing, electronic spread sheets, database managers and graphics programs are all grouped under the title.

A] Browsings Programs.

B] Operating System.

C] Application Software.

D] Data and Information.

Q.23. Keyboard, mouse, monitor, and system unit collectively also known as

A] Solid ware.

B] Software.

C] Hardware.

D] Firm ware.

Q.24. Output of an image on the monitor screen is often called soft copy.

A] True.

B] False.

Q.25. each 0 and 1 in the binary numbering system is called a bit.

A] True.

B] False.

Q.26. Catch memory is used to store most frequently accessed information from the RAM.

A] True.

B] False.

Q.27. The system board is also known as the main board or mother board.

A] True.

B] False.

Q.28. ASSCII, EBCDIC and Unicode are binary coding schemes.

A] True.

B] False.

Q.29. The keys labelled 0-9 on the keyboard are called.

A] Function Keys.

B] Numeric Keys.

C] Typewriter Keys.

D] Special purpose keys.

Q.30. A CD ROM stands for Compact Disk Read Only Memory.

A] True.

B] False.

Q.31. .... consists of step-by-step introductions that tells the computer how to complete the task.

A] Programs.

B] Hardware.

C] Data.

D] Objects.

Q.32. A CD-R stands for CD-Recordable.

A] True.

B] False.

Q.33.......... is a background soft ware that helps the computer to manage its internal resources.

A] System Software.

B] Information.

C] Objects.

D] None of these.

Q.34. Output of an image obtained using a printer is called as hard copy.

A] True.

B] False.

Q.35. Following are the file compression programs, EXCEPT

A] Win Zip.

B] RAID.

C] Win RAR.

D] PK Zip.

Q.36. A track on a disk is one of the many circular ring areas where data is written magnetically.

A] True.

B] False.

Q.37. Floppy disks are removable storage media.

A] True.

B] False.

Q.38. The keyboard keys that have arrows on them are called.

A] Function Keys.

B] Combination Keys.

C] Navigation Keys

D] Special Purpose Keys.

Q.39. Microprocessor is often called as CPU.

A] True.

B] False.

Q.40. Eight bits make up a bite.

A] True.

B] False.

Q.41. Output of an image on the monitor screen is often called hard copy.

A] True.

B] False.

Q.42.......... are graphical objects used to represent and open commonly used applications.

A] G.U.I..

B] Primers'.

C] Windows NT.

D] Icons.

Q.43. A CD-ROM means CD-RW.

A] True.

B] False.

Q.44. Data stored in RAM is

A] Is non-volatile.

B] Is only there while the power is on.

C] Remains only a few minutes after the power is turned off.

D] Is permanent and only lost in power failure.

Q.45. A CD-R stands for CD-Regional.

A] True.

B] False.

Q.46. Primary function of a monitor is to display information to the user.

A] True.

B] False.

Q.47. Random Access Memory] RAM. is .... type of memory.

A] Permanent.

B] Temporary.

C] Flash.

D] Smart.

Q.48 The external memory of the computer is present on the motherboard in the form of slots.

A] False.

B] True.

Q.49 The internal memory of the computer is present on the motherboard in the form of chips

A] True.

B] False.

Q.50 cache memory is used to store most frequently accessed information from the ram.

A] True.

B] False.

Q.1. The "System Date" and "System Time" are the date and time as maintained by the computer's internal clock.

A] True

B] False

Q.2. Disk cleanup is used to rearrange your files so that they are not broken up.

A] True

B] False

Q.3. In Window Vista a folder system is also called a "Directory System."

A] True

B] False

Q.4. "rtf" stands for "rich text format"

A] True

B] False

Q.5. You can click on............. to learn how to use Windows Vista, obtain troubleshooting information, receive support and more.

A] "Search"

B] "Windows"

C] "Start"

D] "Help & Support"

Q.6. In MS paint to draw a curved line, we have to click the.................... Icon.

A] "Curve"

B] "Line"

C] "Polygon"

D] "Rectangle"

Q.7. .... refers to the height and width of the characters to be printed.

A] "Font Size"

B] "Border"

C] "Cell"

D] "Font Style"

Q.8. There is button which is not present on the "Title bar".

A] Minimize

B] Start

C] Maximise

D] Close

Q.9. Disk Defragmenter is used to remove unnecessary files on your hard disk to free up space and your computer run faster.

A] True

B] False

Q.10. To change the size of your picture, Select "Image Attributes" from the menu.

A] True

B] False

Q.11. To start the calculator application click "Start" and select "All Programs Accessories Calculator."

A] True

B] False

Q.12. .... can be used to create and format large and complex text documents.

A] "Calculator"

B] "WordPad"

C] "Notepad"

D] "Text Pad"

Q.13. Notepad is a basic text editor that can be used to create simple documents.

A] True

B] False

Q.14. A folder system is also called a "................"

A] "Direction System"

B] "Directory System"

C] "Directory list"

D] "Folder book"

Q.15. A folder within a folder is known as a "Folder list."

A] True

B] False

Q.17. A .... is like a container in which you can store files.

A] "Icon"

B] "document"

C] "Folder"

D] "Sheet"

Q.18. The operating system's job is .... to

A] Execute many useful commands easily.

B] to make request for service through a defined application programme interface.

C] to control the computer at the most fundamental level.

D] None of these.

Q.19. The windows interface is based on ....

A] "Graphical user Interface" or GUI

B] Application Programme Interface or] API.

C] "Clipboard"

D] None of these

Q.20. The name of a file consists of two parts, the File Name and the sub file name.

A] True

B] False

Q.21. To access the location of the particular file quickly, you create a shortcut icon for the file and place it on the desktop.

A] True

B] False

Q.22. In Windows Vista windows sidebar contains mini-programs called gadgets.

A] True

B] False

Q.23. A file created using Notepad is stored with the extension.................
.

A] ".txt"

B] ".docx"

C] ".png"

D] ".jpg"

Q.1. In MS Word 2007 when text is selected, a "..........." is automatically displayed.

A] Taskbar

B] Main Toolbar

C] Mini Toolbar

D] Menu bar

Q.2. You can make for a TOC using:

A] Heading styles.

B] Custom styles.

C] Outline levels.

D] All of these.

Q.3. .... contains command for opening, saving, printing and closing a file.

A] "Home"

B] "Office Button"

C] "View"

D] "Insert"

Q.4. .... offers a wide variety of options to design documents.

A] Microsoft Excel

B] Microsoft PowerPoint

C] Microsoft Word

D] Microsoft Access

Q.5. All of the following Ribbon tabs are displayed in Word 2007, EXCEPT

A] Home

B] Insert

C] Tools

D] Page Layout

Q.6. When you use the mouse to move the insertion point, the shape of mouse pointer is like I-beam.

A] True

B] False

Q.7. Index shows you at a glance, the topics that are included in the document and make it easier to locate information.

A] True

B] False

Q.8. You can click on the "Format" tab under "WordArt tools" to modify the WordArt as per your requirements.

A] True

B] False

Q.9. In Word, a file is called as a ....

A] "template"

B] "form"

C] "database"

D] "Document"

Q.10. The Mail Marge feature, combines a list of data, typically a file of names and addresses.

A] True

B] False

Q.11. Microsoft Word is the only word processor available in the market.

A] True

B] False

Q.12. Hyperlink identifies a location in the document or a section of text that you name for feature reference.

A] True

B] False

Q.13. A .... is a reference from one part of a document to related information in same another part.

A] Hyperlink

B] Cross-reference

C] Document

D] Linkage

Q.14. For Indentation you may use the "Decrease Indent" and "Increase Indent" icons in the "Paragraph" group on the "............." tab for indenting your text.

A] Insert

B] Home

C] Page Layout

D] Data

Q.15. In MS Word 2007 the "References" tab contains spell check, the squares, and track changes.

A] True

A] False

Q.16. The "..............." is a dictionary of synonyms which you can use to find words that are synonyms with a term.

A] Translate

B] Spelling

C] Thesaurus

D] Research

Q.17. A " .... " is a listing of the topics that appear in a document with their associated page references.

A] Index

B] Table

C] Clipboard

D] Table of contents

Q.18. You can format your document automatically applying styles, available in MS Word 2007.

A] True

B] False

Q.19. A "............." is a connection to a location in the current document to another document or Web Site.

A] Link

B] hyperlink

C] hypolink

D] linkage

Q.20. To view a document in the Print Preview Mode, click on the Office Button and select "Print Print Preview."

A] True

B] False

Q.21. You may use the "The Auto Complete Feature" to automatically correct the grammatical and spelling mistakes in your document.

A] True

B] False

Q.22. Using a word Processing application you can create, modify, store, retrieve and print a document.

A] True

B] False

Q.23. "Mini Toolbar" provides easy way to access the most frequently used formatting commands.

A] True

B] False

Q.24. To print only selected pages in your documnet, you may use either the "Current page" or "Page" option under "Print Range."

A] True

B] False

Q.25. MS Word 2007 when we click on the Office Button the "Edit" menu is displayed.

A] True

B] False

Q.26. A "................" is a pre-designed document useful for creating common purpose documents such as a fax, invoice or business letter.

A] Template

B] File

C] Form

D] Database

Q.27. A multileve list shows the list items at different levels rather then single level.

A] True

B] False

Q.28. A "............" is used to organize information into an easy-to-read format of horizontal rows and vertical columns.

A] Cell

B] Sheet

C] Box

D] Table

Q.29. To remove individual character at the left you may press "............".

A] Delete

B] Backspace

C] Enter

D] Spacebar

Q.30. When you click on "Format Printer" icon on the "Home" tab, you can see that your mouse pointer changes to a "............" icon.

A] paintbrush

B] I-beam

C] Arrow

D] 4-Way arrow

Q.31. You may create a new document using standard templates provided by Word by checking on a template name in the "New Document" window.

A] True

B] False

Q.32. MS Word's Mail Merge feature facilitates you to mail your document about special offers to a large number of people.

A] True

B] False

Q.33. When you move your mouse over a button, a .... is displayed. That provides a detailed description of what the button does.

A] Super-tooltip

B] Sub-tooltip

C] Info

D] Key-tip

Q.34. MS Word 2007 can quickly sort text, data or numbers ascending or descending order.

A] True

B] False

Q.35. .... Applications help you to create different types of written documents such as personal letters, from letters, brochures, faxes and even professional manuals.

A] Word Processor

B] Word Pad

C] Note Pad

D] None of these

Q.36. The "Mailings" tab contains the items required for mail merge.

A] True

B] False

Q.37. Word places footnotes at the end of each page and end notes at the end of documents.

A] True

B] False

Q.38. To remove the hyperlink while retaining the text, right - click on it and select "Remove Hyperlink."

A] True

B] False

Q.39. MS Word indicates formatting inconsistencies with a red wavy underline.

A] True

B] False

Q.40. To automatically correct the document, we use

A] The auto correct feature

B] The auto complete feature

C] Formatting

D] Building Blocks

Q.41. A "..............." is a common application for news paper columns.

A] News reading

B] News letter

C] News

D] News editor

Q.1. In formula bar, an adjacent range is specified by giving the starting and editing cell addresses separated by a

A] Semicolon

B] Comma

C] Full stop

D] Colon

Q.2. The cell address is displayed in the "Text Box".

A] True

B] False

Q.3. A .... is a visual representation of data and conveys the information in an easy to understand and attractive manner.

A] chart

B] table

C] picture

D] graphic

Q.4. In formulas, a non-adjacent range is specified by giving the cell addresses separated by a ....

A] Semicolon

B] Comma

C] Full stop

D] Colon

Q.5. You can use the .... to enter and edit data, instead of editing directly in your work sheet.

A] formula bar

B] title bar

C] menu bar

D] space bar

Q.6. Your Excel 2007 file is stored with the extension "............".

A] ".docx"

B] ".xlsx"

C] ".xltx"

D] ".zltx"

Q.7. In an electronic spreadsheet or worksheet, data can be edited, new data can be added, and unwnated data can be deleted.

A] True

B] False

Q.8. The "Review" tab contains proofing tools like spell check & also has button that let you add comments to a worksheet and manage revisions.

A] True

B] False

Q.9. The "............" tab contains proofing tools like spell check.

A] "Review"

B] "Data"

C] "View"

D] "Insert"

Q.10. You can create and design our own work book templates.

A] True

B] False

Q.11. In a spreadsheet programme as you move from one cell to another, the reference or address to the active cell appears in the "Name Box."

A] True

B] False

Q.12. To start the Microsoft Excel Application, click on the "Start" button and select "All programmes Microsoft Office ? Microsoft Office Excel 2007.

A] True

B] False

Q.13. The "Insert" tab lets you add special ingredients like tables, graphics, charts, and hyperlinks in a spreadsheets programme.

A] True

B] False

Q.14. The text that appears in the bottom margin of the page is called as the "Footer".

A] True

B] False

Q.15. In Excel, a formula always begins with an equal sign] =. and uses arithmetic operators like +, -, *, /, %, and ^ to perform addition, subtraction, multiplication, division, percent and exponentiation respectively.

A] True

B] False

Q.16. While working you may have to reference data from more than one sheet which is called referencing multiple sheets.

A] True

B] False

Q.17. The defalut page orientation setting is "Landscape".

A] True

B] False

Q.18. "............." is a method which aids you in forecasting values.

A] "Find"

B] "Replace"

C] "Goal Seek"

D] "Go to"

Q.19. In MS Excel 2007, below the "Ribbon", we can see Name Box on the left and the Formula Bar on the right.

A] True

B] False

Q.20. A "..............." is a prewritten formula the performs calculations automatically.

A] "Function"

B] "Equation"

C] "Template"

D] "Reaction"

Q.21. MS Excel 2007 is used for different types of .... varying from vary simple to complex.

A] calculations

B] manipulations

C] presentations

D] expressions

Q.22. Your excel file is stored with the extension ".xltx".

A] True

B] False

Q.23. "Autocorrect" is a feature of Microsoft Excel 2007 that makes entering a series of heading easier by logically repeating and extending the series.

A] True

B] False

Q.24. "A relative reference" is a cell or range reference used in a formula whose location does not change when a formula is copied.

A] True

B] False

Q.25. While changing the level of an item in the hierarchy you can increase the indent by using.

A] "Tab"

B] "Backspace"

C] "Delete"

D] "Spacebar"

Q.26. To set margins, select "Margins" from the "Page Setup" group on the "Page Layout" tab.

A] True

B] False

Q.27. To remove individual character at the left you may press "..............".

A] Delete

B] Backspace

C] Enter

D] Spacebar

Q.28. Drop caps are the first character/s at the beginning that are enlarged, conversing several lines.

A] True

B] False

Q.29. The intersection of a row and a column is called a "................".

A] Table

B] Cell

C] Data

D] Sheet

Q.30. A .... is a file that is provided by the application in a "ready to use" format.

A] Sheet

B] Template

C] Book

D] Report

Q.31. A .... is a visual representation of data and conveys the information in a easy to understand and attractive manner.

A] Chart

B] Table

C] Picture

D] Graphic

Q.32. To move among the worksheet in your workbook, you need to click on the "Workbook" tab.

A] True

B] False

Q.33. A theme comprise of a colour palette, font set, and effects.

A] True

B] False

Q.34. You can view two areas of worksheet and lock rows or columns in one area by splitting or freezing panes.

A] True

B] False

Q.35. "..........." are individual designs that can be applied to different parts to the document.

A] "Graphics"

B] "Styles"

C] "Pictures"

D] "Themes"

Q.36. "..........." contains commands for opening, saving, printing, and closing a file.

A] "View" tab

B] "Office Button"

C] "Insert" tab

D] "Review" tab

Q.37. When a formula containing an absolute cell reference is copied to another row or column in the worksheet, the cell reference does not change.

A] True

B] False

Q.38. The "header" is usually the title you give on the page.

A] True

B] False

Q.39. The text that appears in the top margin of the page is called the ....

A] Footer

B] Column

C] Header

D] Paragraph

Q.40. In a spreadsheet programme a table is a selection of two or more cells.

A] True

B] False

Q.41. The "title" is usually given as the footer.

A] True

B] False

Q.42. To stop the automatic relative cell references, i.e. to make the cell reference absolute, type a .... character before the column and row number.

A] # hash.

B] $ dollar.

C] % percent.

D] * star.

Q.43. A theme comprise of a colour palette, font set, and effects.

A] True

B] False

Q.44. To select a group or range of cells, click on the cell you want to begin, drag your cursor and release it when you have reached the end of the selection.

A] True

B] False

Q.45. If we require to add more data to be on one page, we change the page orientation to land scape.

A] True

B] False

Q.46. Each worksheet can be used to organized different types of related information.

A] True

B] False

Q.47. The "table" is a visual representation of data and convey the information in an easy to understand and attractive manner.

A] True

B] False

Q.48. "Themes" provided with MS Excel 2007 are universal designs that unify all of the styles.

A] True

B] False

Q.49. In Microsoft Excel 2007, a single file or document is called a "............".

A] Workbook

B] Worksheet

C] Sheet

D] Notebook

Q.50. "Notebook" contains a collection of one or more worksheets and, optionally, chart sheets containing graphic pictures of your worksheet data.

A] True

B] False

Q.51. With the .... option, you can freeze either or both, rows and columns ie. regardless of where you are in the worksheet you can see the information in these rows and/or columns at all times.

A] Split

B] Arrange

C] Fitter

D] Freeze Panes

Q.52. You can create charts to represent data more effectively in an electronic sheet or worksheet.

A] True

B] False

Q.53. In a spreadsheet each cell has its own address called as "cell address".

A] True

B] False

Q.54. A template file in MS Excel 2007 has an extension "................".

A] .docx

B] .yltx

C] .xltx

D] .zltx

Q.55. A "............" is like an accountant's ledger consisting of rows and columns.

A] Table

B] Microsoft Excel 2007

C] Format

D] Sheet

Q.1. The "Insert" tab contains the basic set of objects which you can insert into a slide.

A] True

B] False

Q.2. Click "Replace All" to replace all occurrences of search text by the specified new text.

A] True

B] False

Q.3. A "................" graphic is a visual representation of your information and ideas.

A] "WordArt"

B] "ClipArt"

C] "SmartArt"

D] "Autoshape"

Q.4. To start a Microsoft PowerPoint Application, click on the "Start" button and select "All progrmmes ? Microsoft Office ? Microsoft Office PowerPoint 2007".

A] True

B] False

Q.5. "..............." refer to a ready-to-use picture.

A] "WordArt"

B] "ClipArt"

C] "SmartArt"

D] "Autoshape"

Q.6. To open a recently used presentation you may click the office button and then click on the presentation name in the list displayed under "Recent Documents".

A] True

B] False

Q.7. SmartArt programs are designed to help you to create an effective presentation.

A] True

B] False

Q.8. The "............." tab contains tools that controls how to slide show is presented.

A] "Design"

B] "Slide Show"

C] "Review"

D] "View"

Q.9. Minature pictures of slides displayed in the slide sorter view.

A] True

B] False

Q.10. .... which displays icon that represent commonly used commands such as Save, Undo, and Redo.

A] Home Button

B] The Ribbon

C] The Quick Access Tool bar

D] The Office Button

Q.11. A "..........." is a connection to a location in the current documnet, another document or a website.

A] Highlink

B] hipolink

C] linkage

D] hyperlink

Q.12. .... are used to create slide shows on the computer

A] Presentation graphics

B] Analytical development programs

C] Super Slide packages

D] Slide maker tools

Q.13. To preview your presentation as web page, you need to add the "Web Page Preview" command to Ribbon.

A] True

B] False

Q.14. With "Slide Show View" you can see how your graphics timings, movies, animated elements and transition effects will look in the actulashow.

A] True

B] False

Q.15. In graphic presentation, programmes each presentation is divided into ....

A] charts

B] slides

C] tables

D] pictures

Q.16. In PowerPoint "Match case": you may check this box for a case sensitive search.

A] True

B] False

Q.17. "Scale to fit paper": check this box to print the slides with an outer frame.

A] True

B] False

Q.18. In PowerPoint "build effects" are animations to slide contents..

A] True

B] False

Q.19. A "..............." is a pre-designed presentation designed for common purpose such as photo album or a quiz show.

A] "Chart"

B] "Table"

C] "Slide"

D] "Template"

Q.20. You may create a new presentation using a template provided by PowerPoint.

A] True

B] False

Q.21. We can insert a video clip on a PowerPoint Slide.

A] True

B] False

Q.22. When you move your mouse over a sizing handle the pointer becomes a ".............".

A] Round Arrow

B] Two-headed Arrow

C] Plus Sign

D] Four-headed Arrow

Q.23. PowerPoint Presentation is a component of following application software.

A] Leap Office

B] Start Office

C] Open Office

D] MS Office

Q.24. "Slide Show View" is an exclusive view of your slides in thumbnail form.

A] True

B] False

Q.25. Headers and Footers are used to add information such as slide numbers, the time and date, a company logo or the presentation title to the top of a hand out or notes page in your presentation, or to bottom of a slide, handout or notes page.

A] True

B] False

Q.26. To see a preview of your slide in a window on the screen, click on the Quick Access Toolbar and select "Print ? Print Preview".

A] True

B] False

Q.27. In Graphics Presentation Programs each presentation is divided into charts.

A] True

B] False

Q.28. Using WordArt graphics, you can effectively communicate your message in a quick and msimple way.

A] True

B] False

Q.29. You may change the presentation views by checking on the buttons displayed on the "..........." at the bottom of the screen.

A] "Title bar"

B] "Menu bar"

C] "Tool bar"

D] "Status bar"

Q.30. "Animations" refers to addition of special visual or sound effect to your slides.

A] True

B] False

Q.31. Using PowerPoint presentation graphics is simple and it is used for effective presentation

A] on a topic.

B] True

C] False

Q.32. A "review" is a way to looking at a presentation.

A] True

B] <u>False</u>

Q.33. In Presentation Graphics "..........." are used to add information such as slide numbers, the time and date, a company logo or the presentation title to the top of a handout or notes page in your presentation, or a bottom of a slide, handout or notes.

A] Hyperlinks

B] Tables

C] <u>Header and Footers</u>

D] Charts

Q.34. The sizing handles at the slides are used to adjust only the height or the width.

A] <u>True</u>

B] False

Q.35. "..............." takes up the full computer screen, like an actual slide show presentation.

A] Slide Sorter View

B] Normal View

C] <u>Slide Show View</u>

D] Notes Page

Q.36. The "Outline" tab shows your slide text in outline form.

A] <u>True</u>

B] False

Q.37. A slide layout refers to the arrangements of elements, such as text, pictures, tables, charts and movies, on a slide.

A] <u>True</u>

B] False

Q.38. If you have a large number of slides in your presentation, you may find it more convenient to use the .... to view all your slides and change their positions.

A] Normal View

B] <u>Slide Sorter View</u>

C] Slide Show View

D] Notes Page

Q.39. You may use either the Normal View or the Slide Sorter View to delete a Slide.

A] True

B] False

Q.40. In Microsoft PowerPoint your file is stored with the .... extension.

A] psd

B] .rtf

C] .pptx

D] .docx

Q.41. When the pointer becomes a ...., you can drag placeholder to the location you wish.

A] Round arrow

B] Two-round arrow

C] Plus sign

D] Four-headed arrow

Q.42. A "Clip" may be a single media file, including art, sound, animation or movies.

A] True

B] False

Q.43. "..........." are details about a file that help identify it.

A] Desktop Properties

B] Window Properties

C] Advanced Properties

D] Document Properties

Q.44. The "Sizing Handles" at the slides and corners of the selection rectangle can be used to adjust the size of the place holder.

A] True

B] False

Q.45. To open a file that you have previously saved, click the Ribbon and select "Open".

A] True

B] False

Q.46. "............." is the main editing view.

A] Slide Sorter View

B] Normal View

C] Slide Show View

D] Notes Page

Q.47. We can insert a audio clip on a powerpoint slide.

A] True

B] False

Q.48. In PowerPoint the "Insert" tab contains tools to design your slides.

A] True

B] False

Q.49. The "..........." tab contains the basic formatting tools.

A] "Design"

B] "View"

C] "Insert"

D] "Home"

Q.50. The "Slides" tab makes it easy to navigate through your presentation and to see the effects of changes and also rearrange, add or delete sliders.

A] True

B] False

Q.1. Netscape Navigator is a type of ....

A] Utility Program.

B] Operating System.

C] Browser.

D] Web Authoring Program.

Q.2. When you type an address such as "http://www.mkcl.org", in this .org indicates.

A] Original Web Site.

B] Commercial Web Site.

C] Organizational Web Site.

D] Educational Web Site.

Q.3. You can search the World Wide Web for a specific topic by using .... and................

A] Gophers, Fido's.

B] Scanner, Search Engine.

C] Search Engines, Indexes.

D Browsers, Larkers.

Q.4. A] n. .... is a set of rules for how information and messages are sent over the internet.

A] Protocol.

B] ISP.

C] Applet.

D] HTML Hyper Text Markup Language.

Q.5. Discussion on the internet about specific topic is known as

A] News.

B] News group.

C] Veronica.

D] Telnet.

Q.6. Which of the following is not a type of protocol?

A] TCI/IP

B] ASCII

C] None of these.

D] ppp

Q.7. Which of the following is a type of protocol?

A] ASCII

B] RAM

C] TCI/IP

D] DBA

Q.8. The three parts of an e-mail message are

A] TCP/IP, Domain and ISP.

B] Destination, Device and Sender.

C] Header, Message and Signature.

D] TCP, IP and Message.

Q.9. The network connecting several computers all over the world is?

A] Intranet.

B] Internet.

C] Arpanet.

D] Network.

Q.10. Which of the following is a browser.

A] Web site.

B] Microsoft.

C] Internet Explorer.

D] www.

Q.11. The terms DNS stands for.

A] Data Naming System.

B] Do Name System.

C] Domain Name System.

D] Duplicate Name System.

Q.12. Internet e-mail address is .... for every user.

A] Unique.

B] Same.

C] Common.

D] None of these.
Q.13. For navigating any website, user has to enter
A] URL.
B] www.
C] PPP.
D] None of these.
Q.14. What is the full form of E-Commerce ?
A] English Commerce.
B] Electronic Commerce.
C] Electric Commerce.
D] Element Commerce.
Q.15. To send e-mail to someone you need ....
A] Resident Address.
B] Internet Connectivity.
C] Fax Address.
D] None of these.
Q.16. .... is used to see the web page.
A] Inbox.
B] Recycle bin.
C] Internet Explorer.
D] Network Neighbourhood.
Q.17. Full form of URL
A] Universal Resource Locator.
B] Uniform Resource Locator.
C] Uni Resource Locator.
D] None of these.
Q.18. Modem converts data from a CD to a hard disk.
A] True.
B] False.
Q.19. Which of the following is a search engine.
A] Google.
B] Alta Vista.
C] Yahoo.
D] All of these.
Q.20. What is meant by E-Commerce?
A] Online selling, purchasing, account handling etc.
B] Subject commerce stream.
C] Electronic equipment to deal with commercial problem.

D] All of the above.

Q.21. . The extensions .gov, .edu, .mil, and .net are called.

A] DNSs.

B] E-mail targets.

C] Domain codes.

D] Mail to address.

Q.22. Web spiders and crawlers are examples of

A] Browsers.

B] Search Engines.

C] HTML Programs.

D] Flames.

Q.23. What is an URL ?

A] A software package used to cruise the World Wide Web..

B] The address of a resource on the World Wide Web.

C] The terms used to describe an internal wizard.

D] A live chat program [Unlimited real time language.

Q.24. What does the abbreviation "www." stands for.

A] World Wide Web.

B] Wide Wide Web.

C] World Width Web.

D] World with Web.

Q.25. Website that allows the user to search for data on keywords is:

A] Chat engines.

B] Routers.

C] Web Server.

D] Search engines.

Q.26. Which of the following web search engine is used worldwide?

A] Domain.

B] Google.

C] Toggle.

D] None of these.

Q.27. When you use a(n) .... to search for a topic, the information you search through is organized into a database like structure.

A] Search engine.

B] Index.

C] Spider.

D] Applet.

Q.28. Which of the following system electronic letter or message sent between individuals or computers.

A] E-mail.

B] Online Service.

C] Share Resources.

D] Voice mail messaging.

Q.29. To add current web to the favourites list.

A] Click "Favourites - Add to Favourites".

B] Click "Add - Favourites.

C] Click "File - Favourites.

D] All of these.

Q.30. Moving around the web from one site to another is referred to as................

A] Linking.

B] Navigating.

C] Hopping.

D] Paging.

Q.31. A protocol defines the rules for passing information between two or more computers.

A] True.

B] False.

Q.32. Information sent over the Internet is divided into small pieces called.

A] Packets.

B] PPPs.

C] e-mail forms.

D] Messages.

Q.33. Protocols like PPP and SLIP are used for.

A] Data Transfer.

B] Dialup internet connection.

C] Domain Registration.

D] None of these.

Q.34. The .com indicates websites of.............. Types of organization.

A] Commercial.

B] Complex.

C] Company.

D] Cargo.

Q.35. Sending messages on the internet to another person's mailbox is

A] E-Business.

B] E-Letter.

C] E-Mail.

D] Cyber Mali.

1. In an unregulated power supply, if load current increases, the output voltage ....

Remains the same

Decreases

Increases

None of the above

Ans : 2

2. In an unregulated power supply, if input a.c. voltage increases, the output

voltage ....

Increases

Decreases

Remains the same

None of the above

Ans : 1

3. A power supply which has voltage regulation of .... is unregulated power

supply

0 %

5 %

10 %

8%

Ans : 3

4. Commercial power supplies have voltage regulation ....

of 10%

of 15%

of 25%

within 1%

Ans : 4

5. An ideal regulated power supply is one which has voltage regulation of ....

0%

5%

10%

1%

Ans : 1

6. A Zener diode utilises .... characteristic for voltage regulation

Forward

Reverse

Both forward and reverse

None of the above

Ans : 2

7. Zener diode can be used as ....

c. voltage regulator only

c. voltage regulator only

both d.c. and a.c. voltage regulator

none of the above

Ans : 3

8. A Zener diode is used as a .... voltage regulating device

Shunt

Series

Series-shunt

None of the above

Ans : 1

9. As the junction temperature increases, the voltage breakdown point for Zener

mechanism ....

Is increased

Is decreased

Remains the same

None of the above

Ans : 2

10. The rupture of co-valent bonds will occur when the electric field is ....

100 V/cm

6 V/cm

1000 V/cm

More than 105 V/cm

Ans : 4

11. In a 15 V Zener diode , the breakdown mechanism will occur by ....

Avalanche mechanism

Zener mechanism

Both Zener and avalanche mechanism

None of the above

Ans : 1

12. A Zener diode that has very narrow depletion layer will breakdown by ....

mechanism

Avalanche

Zener

Both avalanche and Zener

None of the above

Ans : 2

13. As the junction temperature increases, the voltage breakdown point for

avalanche mechanism ....

Remains the same

Decrease

Increases

None of the above

Ans : 3

14. Another name for Zener diode is .... diode

Breakdown

Voltage

Power

Current

Ans : 1

15. Zener diode are generally made of ....

Germanium

Silicon

Carbon

None of the above

Ans : 2

16. For increasing the voltage rating, zeners are connected in ....

Parallel

Series-parallel

Series

None of the above

Ans : 3

17. In a Zener voltage regulator, the changes in load current produce changes

in ....

Zener current

Zener voltage

Zener voltage as well as Zener current

None of the above

Ans : 1

18. A Zener voltage regulator is used for .... load currents

High

Very high

Moderate

Small

Ans : 4

19. A Zener voltage regulator will cease to act as a voltage regulator if Zener

current becomes ....

Less than load current

Zero

More than load current

None of the above

Ans : 2

20. If the doping level is increased, the breakdown voltage of the Zener ....

Remains the same

Is increased

Is decreased

None of the above

Ans : 3

21. A 30 V Zener will have depletion layer width .... that of 10 V Zener

More than

Less than

Equal to

None of the above

Ans : 1

22. The current in a Zener diode is limited by ....

External resistance

Power dissipation
Both (1) and (2)
None of the above
Ans : 3

23. A 5 mA changes in Zener current produces a 50 mA change in Zener voltage.
What is the Zener impedance?
1 O
1 O
100 O
10 O
Ans : 4

24. A certain regulator has a no-load voltage of 6 V and a full-load output of 5.82
V. What is the load regulation?
09%
87 %
72 %
None of the above
Ans : 1

25. What is true about the breakdown voltage in a Zener diode?
It decreases when load current increases
It destroys the diode
It equals current times the resistance
It is approximately constant
Ans : 4

26. Which of these is the best description for a Zener diode?
It is a diode
It is a constant current device
It is a constant-voltage device
It works in the forward region
Ans : 3

27. A Zener diode ....
Is a battery
Acts like a battery in the breakdown region
Has a barrier potential of 1 V
Is forward biased
Ans : 2

28. The load voltage is approximately constant when a Zener diode is ....

Forward biased

Unbiased

Reverse biased

Operating in the breakdown region

Ans : 4

29. In a loaded Zener regulator, which is the largest Zener current?

Series current

Zener current

Load current

None of the above

Ans : 1

30. If the load resistance decreases in a Zener regulator, then Zener current ....

Decreases

Stays the same

Increases

None of the above

Ans : 1

31. If the input a.c. voltage to regulated or ordinary power supply increases by 5%

what will be the approximate change in d.c. output voltage?

10%

20%

15%

5%

Ans : 4

32. If the load current drawn by unregulated power supply increases, the d.c.

output voltage ....

Increases

Decreases

Stays the same

None of the above

Ans : 2

33. If the load current drawn by unregulated power supply increases, the d.c.

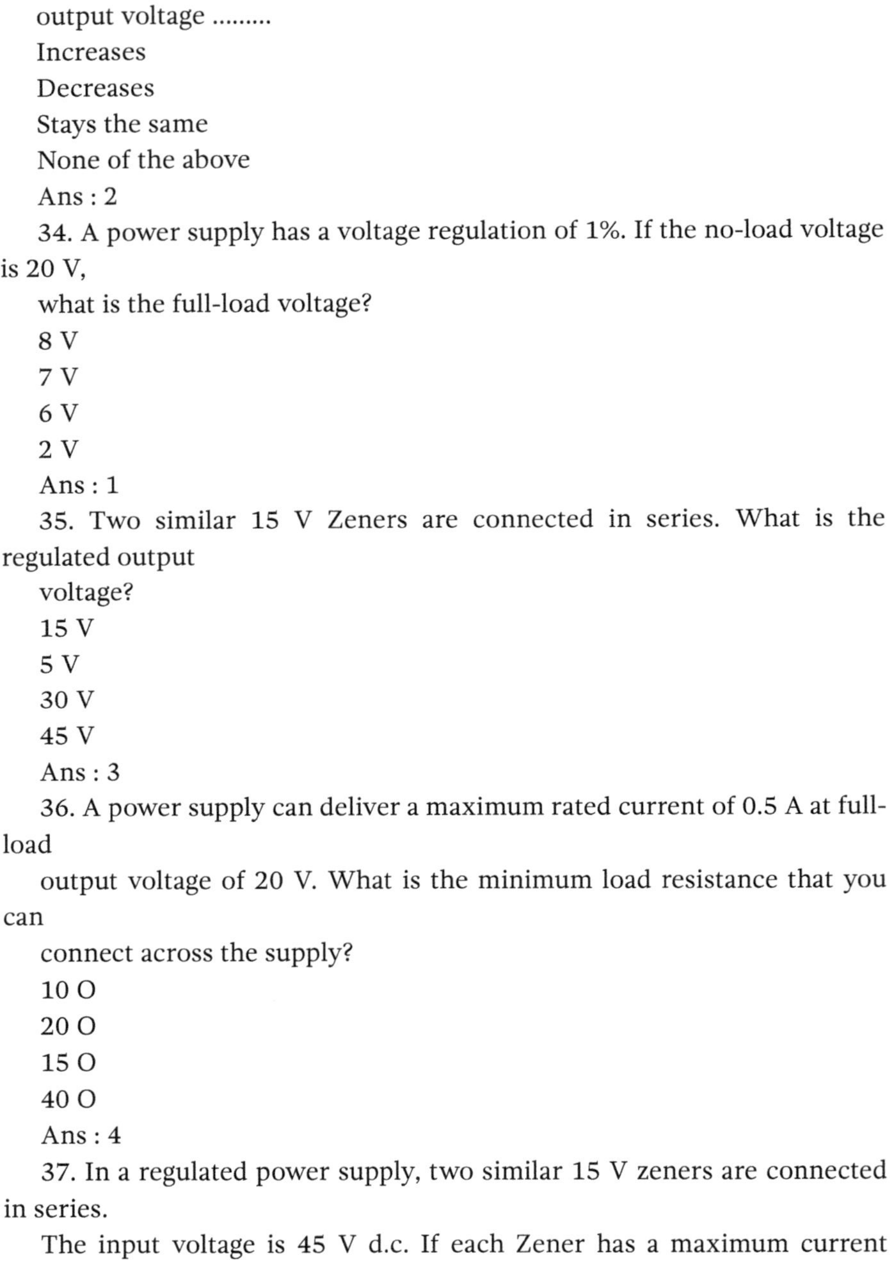

output voltage ....

Increases

Decreases

Stays the same

None of the above

Ans : 2

34. A power supply has a voltage regulation of 1%. If the no-load voltage is 20 V,

what is the full-load voltage?

8 V

7 V

6 V

2 V

Ans : 1

35. Two similar 15 V Zeners are connected in series. What is the regulated output

voltage?

15 V

5 V

30 V

45 V

Ans : 3

36. A power supply can deliver a maximum rated current of 0.5 A at full-load

output voltage of 20 V. What is the minimum load resistance that you can

connect across the supply?

10 O

20 O

15 O

40 O

Ans : 4

37. In a regulated power supply, two similar 15 V zeners are connected in series.

The input voltage is 45 V d.c. If each Zener has a maximum current rating of 300

mA, what should be the value of the series resistance?

10 O

50 O
25 O
40 O
Ans : 2
38. A Zener regulator .... in the power supply
Increases the ripple
Decreases the ripple
Neither increases nor decreases the ripple
Data insufficient
Ans : 2
39. When load current is zero, the Zener current will be ....
Zero
Minimum
Maximum
None of the above
Ans : 3
40. The Zener current will be minimum when ....
Load current is maximum
Load current is minimum
Load current is zero
None of the above
Ans : 1
1. A transistor has ....
A] one pn junction
B] two pn junctions
C] three pn junctions
D] four pn junctions
2. The number of depletion layers in a transistor is ....
A] four
B] three
C] one
D] two
3. The base of a transistor is .... doped
A] heavily
B] moderately
C] lightly
D] none of the above
4. The element that has the biggest size in a transistor is ....

A] collector
B] base
C] emitter
D] collector-base-junction
5. In a pnp transistor, the current carriers are ....
A] acceptor ions
B] donor ions
C] free electrons
D] holes
6. The collector of a transistor is .... doped
A] heavily
B] moderately
C] lightly
D] none of the above
7. A transistor is a .... operated device
A] current
B] voltage
C] both voltage and current
D] none of the above
8. In a npn transistor, ... are the minority carriers
A] free electrons
B] holes
C] donor ions
D] acceptor ions
9. The emitter of a transistor is .... doped
A] lightly
B] heavily
C] moderately
D] none of the above
10. In a transistor, the base current is about .... of emitter current
A] 25%
B] 20%
C] 35 %
D] 5%
11. At the base-emitter junctions of a transistor, one finds ....
A] a reverse bias
B] a wide depletion layer
C] low resistance

D] none of the above

12. The input impedance of a transistor is ....

A] high

B] low

C] very high

D] almost zero

13. Most of the majority carriers from the emitter ....

A] recombine in the base

B] recombine in the emitter

C] pass through the base region to the collector

D] none of the above

14. The current IB is ....

A] electron current

B] hole current

C] donor ion current

D] acceptor ion current

15. In a transistor ....

A] IC = IE + IB

B] IB = IC + IE

C] IE = IC – IB

D] IE = IC + IB

16. The value of a of a transistor is ....

A] more than 1

B] less than 1

C] 1

D] none of the above

17. IC = aIE + ...

A] IB

B] ICEO

C] ICBO

D] ßIB

18. The output impedance of a transistor is ....

A] high

B] zero

C] low

D] very low

19. In a tansistor, IC = 100 mA and IE = 100.2 mA. The value of ß is ....

A] 100
B] 50
C] about 1
D] 200
20. In a transistor if ß = 100 and collector current is 10 mA, then IE is ....
A] 100 mA
B] 100.1 mA
C] 110 mA
D] none of the above
21. The relation between ß and a is ....
A] ß = 1 / (1 – a)
B] ß = (1 – a) / a
C] ß = a / (1 – a)
D] ß = a / (1 + a)
22. The value of ß for a transistor is generally ....
A] 1less than 1
B] between 20 and 500
C] above 500
23. The most commonly used transistor arrangement is .... arrangement
A] common emitter
B] common base
C] common collector
D] none of the above
24. The input impedance of a transistor connected in ....arrangement is the highest
A] common emitter
B] common collector
C] common base
D] none of the above
25. The output impedance of a transistor connected in ....
A] arrangement is the highest
B] common emitter
C] common collector
D] common base
none of the above
26. The phase difference between the input and output voltages in a

common base arrangement is ....

A] 180o

B] 90o

C] 270o

D] 0o

27. The power gain in a transistor connected in .... arrangement is the highest

A] common emitter

B] common base

C] common collector

D] none of the above

28. The phase difference between the input and output voltages of a transistor connected in common emitter arrangement is ....

A] 0o

B] 180o

C] 90o

D] 270o

29. The voltage gain in a transistor connected in .... arrangement is the highest

A] common base

B] common collector

C] common emitter

D] none of the above

30. As the temperature of a transistor goes up, the base-emitter resistance ....

A] decreases

B] increases

C] remains the same

D] none of the above

31. The voltage gain of a transistor connected in common collector

A] arrangement is ....

B] equal to 1

C] more than 10

D] more than 100 less than 1

32. The phase difference between the input and output voltages of a transistor connected in common collector arrangement is ....

A] 180o

B] 0o

C] 90o

D] 270o

33. IC = ß IB + ...

A] ICBO

B] IC

C] <u>ICEO</u>

D] aIE

34. IC = [a / (1 – a)] IB + ...

A] <u>ICEO</u>

B] ICBO

C] IC

D] (1 – a) IB

35. IC = [a / (1 – a)] IB + [........ / (1 – a)]

A] <u>ICBO</u>

B] ICEO

C] IC

D] IE

36. BC 147 transistor indicates that it is made of ....

A] germanium

B] <u>silicon</u>

C] carbon

D] none of the above

37. ICEO = (.........) ICBO

A] ß1

B] + a

C] <u>1 + ß</u>

D] none of the above

38. A transistor is connected in CB mode. If it is not connected in CE mode with same bias voltages, the values of IE, IB and IC will ....

A] <u>remain the same</u>

B] increase

C] decrease

D] none of the above

39. If the value of a is 0.9, then value of ß is ....

A] 9

B] 0.9

C] 900

D] <u>90</u>

40. In a transistor, signal is transferred from a .... circuit

A] high resistance to low resistance

B] low resistance to high resistance

C] high resistance to high resistance

D] low resistance to low resistance

41. The arrow in the symbol of a transistor indicates the direction of ....

A] electron current in the emitter

B] electron current in the collector

C] hole current in the emitter

D] donor ion current

42. The leakage current in CE arrangement is .... that in CB arrangement

A] more than

B] less than

C] the same as

D] none of the above

43. A heat sink is generally used with a transistor to ....

A] increase the forward current

B] decrease the forward current

C] compensate for excessive doping

D] prevent excessive temperature rise

44. The most commonly used semiconductor in the manufacture of a transistor is ....

A] germanium

B] silicon

C] carbon

D] none of the above

45. The collector-base junction in a transistor has ....

A] forward bias at all times

B] reverse bias at all times

C] low resistance

D] none of the above

1. Transistor biasing represents .... conditions

1. a.c.

2. d.c.

3. both a.c. and d.c.

4. none of the above

Ans : 2

2. Transistor biasing is done to keep ………… in the circuit

Proper direct current

Proper alternating current

The base current small

Collector current small

Ans : 1

3. Operating point represents …………..

Values of IC and VCE when signal is applied

The magnitude of signal

Zero signal values of IC and VCE

None of the above

Ans : 3

TRANSISTOR BIASING Questions and Answers pdf

4. If biasing is not done in an amplifier circuit, it results in ……………

Decrease in the base current

Unfaithful amplification

Excessive collector bias

None of the above

Ans : 2

5. Transistor biasing is generally provided by a …………….

Biasing circuit

Bias battery

Diode

None of the above

Ans : 1

6. For faithful amplification by a transistor circuit, the value of VBE should ………. for a silicon transistor

Be zero

Be 0.01 V

Not fall below 0.7 V

Be between 0 V and 0.1 V

Ans : 3

7. For proper operation of the transistor, its collector should have …………

Proper forward bias

Proper reverse bias

Very small size

None of the above

Ans : 2

8. For faithful amplification by a transistor circuit, the value of VCE should .... for silicon transistor

Not fall below 1 V

Be zero

Be 0.2 V

None of the above

Ans : 1

9. The circuit that provides the best stabilization of operating point is ....

Base resistor bias

Collector feedback bias

Potential divider bias

None of the above

Ans : 3

10. The point of intersection of d.c. and a.c. load lines represents ....

Operating point

Current gain

Voltage gain

None of the above

Ans : 1

11. An ideal value of stability factor is ....

100

200

More than 200

1

Ans : 4

12. The zero signal IC is generally .... mA in the initial stages of a transistor amplifier

41

3

More than 10

Ans : 2

13. If the maximum collector current due to signal alone is 3 mA, then zero signal collector current should be at least equal to ....

6 mA

mA
3 mA
1 mA
Ans : 3
14. The disadvantage of base resistor method of transistor biasing is that it …………
Is complicated
Is sensitive to changes in ß
Provides high stability
None of the above
Ans : 2
15. The biasing circuit has a stability factor of 50. If due to temperature change, ICBO changes by 1 µA, then IC will change by …………
100 µA
25 µA
20 µA
50 µA
Ans : 4
16. For good stabilsation in voltage divider bias, the current I1 flowing through R1 and R2 should be equal to or greater than
10 IB
3 IB
2 IB
4 IB
Ans : 1
17. The leakage current in a silicon transistor is about ………… the leakage current in a germanium transistor
One hundredth
One tenth
One thousandth
One millionth
Ans : 3
18. The operating point is also called the ………….
Cut off point
Quiescent point
Saturation point

None of the above
Ans : 2
19. For proper amplification by a transistor circuit, the operating point should be located at the .... of the d.c. load line
The end point
Middle
The maximum current point
None of the above
Ans : 2
20. The operating point .... on the a.c. load line
Also line
Does not lie
May or may not lie
Data insufficient
Ans : 1
21. The disadvantage of voltage divider bias is that it has ....
High stability factor
Low base current
Many resistors
None of the above
Ans : 3
22. Thermal runaway occurs when ....
Collector is reverse biased
Transistor is not biased
Emitter is forward biased
Junction capacitance is high
Ans : 2
23. The purpose of resistance in the emitter circuit of a transistor amplifier is to ....
Limit the maximum emitter current
Provide base-emitter bias
Limit the change in emitter current
None of the above
Ans : 3
24. In a transistor amplifier circuit VCE = VCB + ...
VBE
2VBE
5 VBE

None of the above

Ans : 1

25. The base resistor method is generally used in ....

Amplifier circuits

Switching circuits

Rectifier circuits

None of the above

Ans : 2

26. For germanium transistor amplifier, VCE should .... for faithful amplification

Be zero

Be 0.2 V

Not fall below 0.7 V

None of the above

Ans : 3

27. In a base resistor method, if the value of ß changes by 50, then collector current will change by a factor ....

25

50

100

200

Ans : 2

28. The stability factor of a collector feedback bias circuit is .... that of base resistor bias.

The same as

More than

Less than

None of the above

Ans : 3

29. In the design of a biasing circuit, the value of collector load RC is determined by ....

VCE consideration

VBE consideration

IB consideration

None of the above

Ans : 1

30. If the value of collector current IC increases, then the value of VCE ....

Remains the same
Decreases
Increases
None of the above
Ans : 2
31. If the temperature increases, the value of VCE ....
Remains the same
Is increased
Is decreased
None of the above
Ans : 3
32. The stabilisation of operating point in potential divider method is provided by ....
RE consideration
RC consideration
VCC consideration
None of the above
Answer: 1
33. The value of VBE ....
Depends upon IC to moderate extent
Is almost independent of IC
Is strongly dependant on IC
None of the above
Ans : 2
34. When the temperature changes, the operating point is shifted due to ....
Change in ICBO
Change in VCC
Change in the values of circuit resistance
None of the above
Ans : 1
35. The value of stability factor for a base resistor bias is ....
RB (ß+1)
(ß+1)RC
(ß+1)
1-ß
Ans : 3
36. In a particular biasing circuit, the value of RE is about ....

10 kO

1 MO

100 kO

800 O

Ans : 4

37. A silicon transistor is biased with base resistor method. If ß=100, VBE =0.7 V, zero signal collector current IC = 1 mA and VCC = 6V , what is the value of the base resistor RB?

105 kO

530 kO

315 kO

None of the above

Ans : 2

38. In voltage divider bias, VCC = 25 V; R1 = 10 kO; R2 = 2.2 V ; RC = 3.6 V and RE =1 kO. What is the emitter voltage?

7 V

3 V

V8

V

Ans : 4

39. In the above question (Q38.) , what is the collector voltage?

3 V

8 V

6 V

7 V

Ans : 1

40. In voltage divider bias, operating point is 3 V, 2 mA. If VCC = 9 V, RC = 2.2 kO, what is the value of RE ?

2000 O

1400 O

800 O

1600 O

Ans : 3

1. A tuned amplifier uses .... load

A] Resistive

B] Capacitive

C] <u>LC tank</u>

D] Inductive

2. A tuned amplifier is generally operated in .... operation
A] Class A
B] Class C
C] Class B
D] None of the above
3. A tuned amplifier is used in .... applications
A] Radio frequency
B] Low frequency
C] Audio frequency
D] None of the above
4. Frequencies above .... kHz are called radio frequencies
A] 21
B] 0
C] 50
D] 200
6. The voltage gain of a tuned amplifier is .... at resonant frequency
A] Minimum
B] Maximum
C] Half-way between maximum and minimum
D] Zero
7. At parallel resonance, the line current is ....
A] Minimum
B] Maximum
C] Quite large
D] None of the above
8. At series resonance, the circuit offers .... impedance
A] Zero
B] Maximum
C] Minimum
D] None of the above
9. A resonant circuit contains .... elements
A] R and L only
B] R and C only
C] Only R
D] L and C
10. At series or parallel resonance, the circuit behaves as a .... load
A] Capacitive
B] Resistive

C] Inductive

D] None of the above

11. At series resonance, voltage across L is .... voltage across C

A] Equal to but opposite in phase to

B] Equal to but in phase with

C] Greater than but in phase with

D] Less than but in phase with

12. When either L or C is increased, the resonant frequency of LC circuit ....

A] Remains the same

B] Increases

C] Decreases

D] Insufficient data

13. At parallel resonance, the net reactive component circuit current is ....

A] Capacitive

B] Zero

C] Inductive

D] None of the above

14. In parallel resonance, the circuit impedance is ....

A] C/LR

B] R/LC

C] CR/L

D] L/CR

15. In a parallel LC circuit, if the input signal frequency is increased above resonant frequency then ....

A] XL increases and XC decreases

B] XL decreases and XC increases

C] Both XL and XC increase

D] Both XL and XC decrease

16. The Q of an LC circuit is given by ....

A] 2pfr x R

B] R / 2pfrL

C] 2pfrL / R

D] R2/2pfrL

17. If Q of an LC circuit increases, then bandwidth ....

A] Increases

B] Decreases

C] Remains the same

D] Insufficient data

18. At series resonance, the net reactive component of circuit current is ....

A] Zero

B] Inductive

C] Capacitive

D] None of the above

19. The dimensions of L/CR are that of ....

A] Farad

B] Henry

C] Ohm

D] None of the above

20. If L/C ratio of a parallel LC circuit is increased, the Q of the circuit ....

A] Is decreased

B] Is increased

C] Remains the same

D] None of the above

21. At series resonance, the phase angle between applied voltage and circuit is ....

A] 90o

B] 180o

C] 0o

D] None of the above

22. At parallel resonance, the ratio L/C is ....

A] Very large

B] Zero

C] Small

D] None of the above

23. If the resistance of a tuned circuit is increased, the Q of the circuit ....

A] Is increased

B] Is decreased

C] Remains the same

D] None of the above

24. The Q of a tuned circuit refers to the property of ....

A] Sensitivity

B] Fidelity

C] Selectivity

D] None of the above

25. At parallel resonance, the phase angle between the applied voltage and circuit current is ....

A] 90o

B] 180o

C] 0o

D] None of the above

26. In a parallel LC circuit, if the signal frequency is decreased below the resonant frequency, then ....

A] XL decreases and XC increases

B] XL increases and XC decreases

C] Line current becomes minimum

D] None of the above

27. In series resonance, there is ....

A] Voltage amplification

B] Current amplification

C] Both voltage and current amplification

D] None of the above

28. The Q of a tuned amplifier is generally ....

A] Less than 5

B] Less than 10

C] More than 10

D] None of the above

29. The Q of a tuned amplifier is 50. If the resonant frequency for the amplifier is 1000kHZ, then bandwidth is ....

A] 10kHz

B] 40 kHz

C] 30 kHz

D] 20 kHz

30. In the above question, what are the values of cut-off frequencies?

A] 140 kHz , 60 kHz

B] 1020 kHz , 980 kHz

C] 1030 kHz , 970 kHz

D] None of the above

31. For frequencies above the resonant frequency, a parallel LC circuit behaves as a .... load

A] Capacitive
B] Resistive
C] Inductive
D] None of the above

32. In parallel resonance, there is ....
A] Both voltage and current amplification
B] Voltage amplifications
C] Current amplification
D] None of the above

33. For frequencies below resonant frequency, a series LC circuit behaves as a .... load
A] Resistive
B] Capacitive
C] Inductive
D] None of the above

34. If a high degree of selectivity is desired, then double-tuned circuit should have .... coupling
A] Loose
B] Tight
C] Critical
D] None of the above

35. In the double tuned circuit, if the mutual inductance between the two tuned circuits is decreased, the level of resonance curve ....
A] Remains the same
B] Is lowered
C] Is raised
D] None of the above

36. For frequencies above the resonant frequency , a series LC circuit behaves as a .... load
A] Resistive
B] Inductive
C] Capacitive
D] None of the above

37. Double tuned circuits are used in .... stages of a radio receiver
A] IF
B] Audio
C] Output
D] None of the above

38. A class C amplifier always drives .... load

A] A pure resistive

B] A pure inductive

C] A pure capacitive

D] A resonant tank

39. Tuned class C amplifiers are used for RF signals of ....

A] Low power

B] High power

C] Very high power

D] None of the above

40. For frequencies below the resonant frequency , a parallel LC circuit behaves as a .... load

A] Inductive

B] Resistive

C] Capacitive

D] None of the above

1. A radio receiver has .... of amplification

A] One stage

B] Two stages

C] Three stages

D] More than one stages

2. RC coupling is used for .... amplification

A] Voltage

B] Current

C] Power

D] None of the above

3. In an RC coupled amplifier, the voltage gain over mid-frequency range ....

A] Changes abruptly with frequency

B] Is constant

C] Changes uniformly with frequency

D] None of the above

4. In obtaining the frequency response curve of an amplifier, the ....

A] Amplifier level output is kept constant

B] Amplifier frequency is held constant

C] Generator frequency is held constant

D] Generator output level is held constant

5. An advantage of RC coupling scheme is the ....Good impedance matching

A] Economy

B] High efficiency

C] None of the above

6. The best frequency response is of .... coupling

A] RC

B] Transformer

C] Direct

D] None of the above

7. Transformer coupling is used for .... amplification

A] Power

B] Voltage

C] Current

D] None of the above

8. In an RC coupling scheme, the coupling capacitor CC must be large enough ....

A] To pass d.c. between the stages

B] Not to attenuate the low frequencies

C] To dissipate high power

D] None of the above

9. In RC coupling, the value of coupling capacitor is about ....

A] 100 pF

B] 0.1 μF

C] 0.01 μF

D] 10 μF

11. When a multistage amplifier is to amplify d.c. signal, then one must use .... coupling

A] RC

B] Transformer

C] Direct

D] None of the above

12. .... coupling provides the maximum voltage gain

A] RC

B] Transformer

C] Direct

D] Impedance

13. In practice, voltage gain is expressed ....

A] In db
B] In volts
C] As a number
D] None of the above

14. Transformer coupling provides high efficiency because ....
A] Collector voltage is stepped up
B] resistance is low
C] collector voltage is stepped down
D] none of the above

15. Transformer coupling is generally employed when load resistance is ....
A] Large
B] Very large
C] Small
D] None of the above

16. If a three-stage amplifier has individual stage gains of 10 db, 5 db and 12 db, then total gain in db is ....
A] 600 db
B] 24 db
C] 14 db
D] 27 db

17. The final stage of a multistage amplifier uses ....
A] RC coupling
B] Transformer coupling
C] Direct coupling
D] Impedance coupling

18. The ear is not sensitive to ....
A] Frequency distortion
B] Amplitude distortion
C] Frequency as well as amplitude distortion
D] None of the above

19. RC coupling is not used to amplify extremely low frequencies because ....
A] There is considerable power loss
B] There is hum in the output
C] Electrical size of coupling capacitor becomes very large
D] None of the above

20. In transistor amplifiers, we use .... transformer for impedance matching

A] Step up

B] Step down

C] Same turn ratio

D] None of the above

21. The lower and upper cut off frequencies are also called .... frequencies

A] Sideband

B] Resonant

C] Half-resonant

D] Half-power

22. A gain of 1,000,000 times in power is expressed by ....

A] 30 db

B] 60 db

C] 120 db

D] 600 db

23. A gain of 1000 times in voltage is expressed by ....

A] 60 db

B] 30 db

C] 120 db

D] 600 db

24. 1 db corresponds to .... change in power level

A] 50%

B] 35%

C] 26%

D] 22%

25. 1 db corresponds to .... change in voltage or current level

A] 40%

B] 80%

C] 20%

D] 25%

26. The frequency response of transformer coupling is ....

A] Good

B] Very good

C] Excellent

D] Poor

27. In the initial stages of a multistage amplifier, we use ....

A] RC coupling

B] Transformer coupling

C] Direct coupling

D] None of the above

28. The total gain of a multistage amplifier is less than the product of the gains of individual stages due to ....

A] Power loss in the coupling device

B] Loading effect of the next stage

C] The use of many transistors

D] The use of many capacitors

29. The gain of an amplifier is expressed in db because ....

A] It is a simple unit

B] Calculations become easy

C] Human ear response is logarithmic

D] None of the above

30. If the power level of an amplifier reduces to half, the db gain will fall by ....

A] 5 db

B] 2 db

C] 10 db

D] 3 db

31. A current amplification of 2000 is a gain of ....

A] 3 db

B] 66 db

C] 20 db

D] 200 db

32. An amplifier receives 0.1 W of input signal and delivers 15 W of signal power. What is the power gain in db?

A] 8 db

B] 6 db

C] 5 db

D] 4 db

33. The power output of an audio system is 18 W. For a person to notice an increase in the output (loudness or sound intensity) of the system, what must the output power be increased to ?

A] 2 W

B] 6 W

C] 68 W

D] None of the above

34. The output of a microphone is rated at -52 db. The reference level is 1V under specified conditions. What is the output voltage of this microphone under the same sound conditions?

A] 5 mV

B] 2 mV

C] 8 mV

D] 5 mV

35. RC coupling is generally confined to low power applications because of ....

A] Large value of coupling capacitor

B] Low efficiency

C] Large number of components

D] None of the above

36. The number of stages that can be directly coupled is limited because ....

A] Changes in temperature cause thermal instability

B] Circuit becomes heavy and costly

C] It becomes difficult to bias the circuit

D] None of the above

37. The purpose of RC or transformer coupling is to ....

A] Block a.c.

B] Separate bias of one stage from another

C] Increase thermal stability

D] None of the above

38. The upper or lower cut off frequency is also called ....frequency

A] Resonant

B] Sideband

C] 3 db

D] None of the above

39. The bandwidth of a single stage amplifier is .... that of a multistage amplifier

A] More than

B] The same as

C] Less than

D] Data insufficient

40. The value of emitter capacitor CE in a multistage amplifier is about ....

A] 1 μF
B] 100 pF
C] 0.01 μF
D] <u>50 μF</u>
1. An oscillator converts ....
c. power into d.c. power
c. power into a.c. power
mechanical power into a.c. power
none of the above
Answer : 2
2. In an LC transistor oscillator, the active device is ....
LC tank circuit
Biasing circuit
Transistor
None of the above
Answer : 3
3. In an LC circuit, when the capacitor is maximum, the inductor energy is ....
Minimum
Maximum
Half-way between maximum and minimum
None of the above
Answer : 1
4. In an LC oscillator, the frequency of oscillator is .... L or C.
Proportional to square of
Directly proportional to
Independent of the values of
Inversely proportional to square root of
Answer : 4
5. An oscillator produces................ oscillations
Damped
Undamped
Modulated
None of the above
Answer : 2
6. An oscillator employs .... feedback
Positive
Negative

Neither positive nor negative
Data insufficient
Answer : 1
7. An LC oscillator cannot be used to produce .... frequencies
High
Audio
Very low
Very high
Answer : 3
8. Hartley oscillator is commonly used in ....
Radio receivers
Radio transmitters
TV receivers
None of the above
Answer : 1
9. In a phase shift oscillator, we use .... RC sections
Two
Three
Four
None of the above
Answer : 2
10. In a phase shift oscillator, the frequency determining elements are ....
L and C
R, L and C
R and C
None of the above
Answer : 3
11. A Wien bridge oscillator uses .... feedback
Only positive
Only negative
Both positive and negative
None of the above
Answer : 3
12. The piezoelectric effect in a crystal is ....
A voltage developed because of mechanical stress
A change in resistance because of temperature
A change in frequency because of temperature

None of the above

Answer : 1

13. If the crystal frequency changes with temperature, we say that crystal

has .... temperature coefficient

Positive

Zero

Negative

None of the above

Answer : 1

14. The crystal oscillator frequency is very stable due to .... of the crystal

Rigidity

Vibrations

Low Q

High Q

Answer : 4

15. The application where one would most likely find a crystal oscillator is ....

Radio receiver

Radio transmitter

AF sweep generator

None of the above

Answer : 2

16. An oscillator differs from an amplifier because it ....

Has more gain

Requires no input signal

Requires no d.c. supply

Always has the same input

Answer : 2

17. One condition for oscillation is ....

A phase shift around the feedback loop of 180o

A gain around the feedback loop of one-third

A phase shift around the feedback loop of 0o

A gain around the feedback loop of less than 1

Answer : 3

18. A second condition for oscillations is ....

A gain of 1 around the feedback loop

No gain around the feedback loop

The attention of the feedback circuit must be one-third

The feedback circuit must be capacitive

Answer : 1

19. In a certain oscillator Av = 50. The attention of the feedback circuit must

be ....

1

01

10

02

Answer : 4

20. For an oscillator to properly start, the gain around the feedback loop must

initially be

1

Greater than 1

Less than 1

Equal to attenuation of feedback circuit

Answer : 2

21. In a Wien-bridge oscillator, if the resistances in the positive feedback circuit

are decreased, the frequency..........

Remains the same

Decreases

Increases

Insufficient data

Answer : 3

22. In Colpitt's oscillator, feedback is obtained ....

By magnetic induction

By a tickler coil

From the centre of split capacitors

None of the above

Answer : 3

23. The Q of the crystal is of the order of ....

100

1000

50

More than 10,000

Answer : 4

24. Quartz crystal is most commonly used in crystal oscillators because ....

It has superior electrical properties

It is easily available

It is quite inexpensive

None of the above

Answer : 1

27. .... is a fixed frequency oscillator

Phase-shift oscillator

Hartely-oscillator

Colpitt's oscillator

Crystal oscillator

Answer : 4

28. In an LC oscillator, if the value of L is increased four times, the frequency of

oscillations is ....

Increased 2 times

Decreased 4 times

Increased 4 times

Decreased 2 times

Answer : 4

29. An important limitation of a crystal oscillator is ....

Its low output

Its high Q

Less availability of quartz crystal

Its high output

Answer : 1

30. The signal generator generally used in the laboratories is .... oscillator

Wien-bridge

Hartely

Crystal

Phase shift

Answer : 1

1.In which of the following base systems is 123 not a valid number?

(a) Base 10

(b) Base 16

(c)Base8

(d) Base 3

2. Storage of 1 KB means the following number of bytes

(a) 1000

(b)964

(c)1024

(d) 1064

3. What is the octal equivalent of the binary number:

10111101

(a)675

(b)275

(c) 572

(d) 573.

4. Pick out the CORRECT statement:

(a) In a positional number system, each symbol represents the same value irrespective of its position

(b) The highest symbol in a position number system as a value equal to the number of symbols in the system

(c) It is not always possible to find the exact binary

(d) Each hexadecimal digit can be represented as a sequence of three binary symbols.

5.The binary code of (21.125)10 is

(a) 10101.001

(b) 10100.001

(c) 10101.010

(d) 10100.111.

6.A NAND gate is called a universal logic element because

(a) it is used by everybody

(b) any logic function can be realized by NAND gates alone

(c) all the minization techniques are applicable for optimum NAND gate realization

(d) many digital computers use NAND gates.

7. Digital computers are more widely used as compared to analog computers,

because they are

(a) less expensive

(b) always more accurate and faster

(c) <u>useful over wider ranges of problem types</u>

(d) easier to maintain.

8. Most of the digital computers do not have floating point hardware because

(a) <u>floating point hardware is costly</u>

(b) it is slower than software

(c) it is not possible to perform floating point addition by hardware

(d) of no specific reason.

9. The number 1000 would appear just immediately after

(a) FFFF (hex)

(b) 1111 (binary)

(c) 7777 (octal)

(d) <u>All of the above.</u>

10. (1(10101)2 is

(a) <u>(37)10</u>

(b) (69)10

(c) (41)10

(d) — (5)10

11. The number of Boolean functions that can be generated by n variables is equal to

(a) 2n

(b) <u>22 n</u>

(c) 2n-1

(d) — 2n

12. Consider the representation of six-bit numbers by two's complement, one's complement, or by sign and magnitude: In which representation is there overflow from the addition of the integers 011000 and 011000?

(a) Two's complement only

(b) Sign and magnitude and one's complement only

(c) Two's complement and one's complement only

(d) <u>All three representations.</u>

13. A hexadecimal odometer displays F 52 F. The next reading will be

(a)F52E

(b)G52F

(c)F53F

(d)<u>F53O.</u>

14. Positive logic in a logic circuit is one in which

(a) logic 0 and 1 are represented by 0 and positive voltage respectively

(b) logic 0 and, -1 are represented by negative and positive voltages respectively

(c) logic 0 voltage level is higher than logic 1 voltage level

(d) logic 0 voltage level is lower than logic 1 voltage level.

15. Which of the following gate is a two-level logic gate

(a) OR gate

(b) NAND gate

(c) EXCLUSIVE OR gate

(d) NOT gate.

16. Among the logic families, the family which can be used at very high frequency greater than 100 MHz in a 4 bit synchronous counter is

(a) TTLAS

(b) CMOS

(c)ECL

(d)TTLLS

17. An AND gate will function as OR if

(a) all the inputs to the gates are "1"

(b) all the inputs are '0'

(c) either of the inputs is "1"

(d) all the inputs and outputs are complemented.

18. An OR gate has 6 inputs. The number of input words in its truth table are

(a)6

(b)32

(c) 64

(d) 128

19. A debouncing circuit is

(a) an astable MV

(b) a bistable MV

(c) a latch

(d) a monostable MV.

20. NAND. gates are preferred over others because these

(a) have lower fabrication area

(b) can be used to make any gate

(c) consume least electronic power

(d) provide maximum density in a chip.

21. In case of OR gate, no matter what the number of inputs, a

(a) 1 at any input causes the output to be at logic 1

(b) 1 at any input causes the output to be at logic 0

(c) 0 any input causes the output to be at logic 0

(d) 0 at any input causes the output to be at logic 1.

22. The fan put of a 7400 NAND gate is

(a)2TTL

(b)5TTL

(c)8TTL

(d)10TTL

23. Excess-3 code is known as

(a) Weighted code

(b) Cyclic redundancy code

(c) Self-complementing code

(d) Algebraic code.

k24. Assuming 8 bits for data, 1 bit for parity, I start bit and 2 stop bits, the number of characters that 1200 BPS communication line can transmit is

(a)10 CPS

(b)120 CPS

(c) 12CPS

(d) None of the above.

www.ingramcontent.com/pod-product-compliance
Ingram Content Group UK Ltd.
Pitfield, Milton Keynes, MK11 3LW, UK
UKHW021907190726
13853UKWH00002B/554